→THE GOSPEL IN CYBERSPACE

Nurturing Faith in the Internet Age

→THE GOSPEL IN CYBERSPACE

Nurturing Faith in the Internet Age

Pierre Babin
Angela Ann Zukowski

Cover, pages iii, 2, 23, 123, 173: Bill Brooks/Masterfile

Cover and Interior Design: Lucy Lesiak/Lucy Lesiak Design

Library of Congress Cataloging-in-Publication Data

Babin, Pierre.
    [Médias chance pour l'évangile. French]
    The gospel in cyberspace : nurturing faith in the internet age / Pierre Babin,
Angela Ann Zukowski.
      p. cm.
    Includes bibliographical references.
    ISBN 0-8294-1740-0
    1. Evangelistic work. 2. Internet (Computer network)—Religious aspects—
Christianity. I. Zukowski, Angela Ann. II. Title.

BV3793 .B2313 2001
261.5′2—dc21   2001038545

ISBN: 0-8294-1740-0

Published by Loyola Press, 3441 N. Ashland Avenue, Chicago, Illinois 60657 U.S.A.

01 02 03 04 05 Bang 5 4 3 2 1

Table of Contents

Preface

We intend this book to be a living example of the ways to evangelize at the dawn of the twenty-first century, in three ways:

- It is the fruit of a dialogue between two quite different persons: Angela Ann Zukowski and Pierre Babin, a woman and a man, an American and a Frenchman.

- It has been written in the marketplace of the world. Both of the authors direct institutes of training in communication, ecumenical and international centers where people from 120 countries of the world have come to be trained. We speak several languages and have given training sessions on five continents. We believe in the advent of the "global village."

- Still more than a sharing of ideas, this book expresses the sharing of our deepest goods: what makes us live, "the hidden treasure" in our innermost being, our convictions built all along the years. Such is our common thought: in the era of the media and of Internet, evangelizing is a dialogue on the marketplace of the world to share our spiritual riches.

We have intended an original book, a book with a redactional form fitting the spoken words. Rather than a thesis with chapters in good order, it appears to you as a kaleidoscope of our convictions, a mosaic which is neither a muddle nor an exchange of witty remarks around a cup of tea. You will find in the kaleidoscope two basic colors reflecting the sensitivity of each author. In the first and third parts Angela Ann Zukowski (green and red?) states firmly her faith in a mixing between Gospel and new technologies, between the theological tradition and the New Age. In the second part Pierre Babin (the blue of Chartres stained glass?) tries to break open the universe of the media to perceive in it the affinities with the Gospel, the incredible possibilities for our time but also the dangers and the conditions.

Why three parts and not an alternation of questions and answers? The reader, in our opinion, should perceive our exchange better if he or she encounters two well-defined patterns of thinking, each with its unique way of expression. The Gutenberg age of print offers something good in holding us to precision and coordination of ideas; nevertheless the future belongs to multimedia! Besides, the presentation of the book in sections does not hamper the freedom in writing, the shifting balances and unexpected new developments. Finally, an epilogue in the form of an interview presents a conversation about the key points of the respective messages.

Is there a unity between us? Indeed—the fundamental unity of a positive outlook on this world, on the opportunities of the new technologies. For us it is impossible to believe in God without believing in the human being and without promoting positively the human inventions.

Aware as we are of being involved in a major turning point of civilization, we would like to share our outlook and our faith. We are convinced that under the influence of the new technologies a new civilization is seeking itself. "I am not pessimistic," said McLuhan, "I am apocalyptic." He wanted to be an enlightener. We think that another way of being human, more universal, more oriented toward dialogue, freer, could emerge from the profusion of electronic technologies. We believe that at the center of that future civilization could emerge a humanity better aware of its inner, spiritual, and mysterious source. Rather than decrying and criticizing, we think that the best way to exorcise the dangers of the "New Age" is to embark with the Gospel in our hands.

May you, the reader, wander through these chapters as in a forest! May every tree, every view become for you a surprise nourishing your own conversation.

Angela Ann Zukowski
Pierre Babin

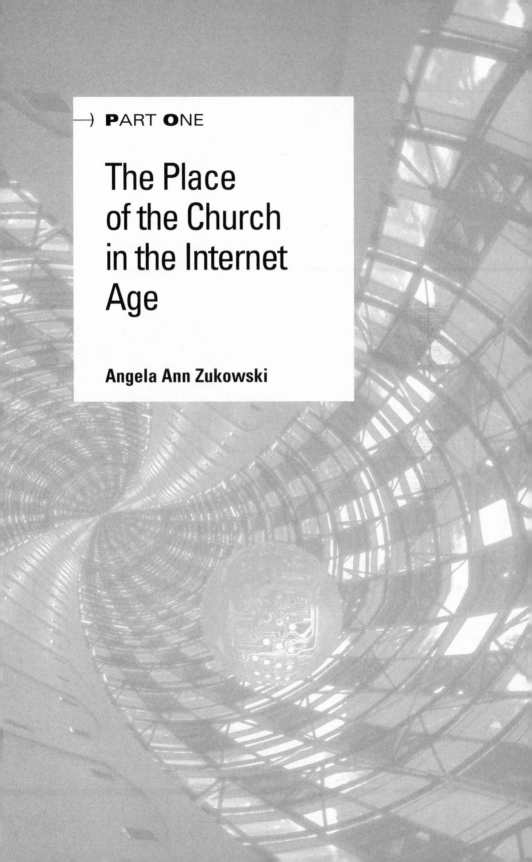

—) **P**ART **O**NE

The Place
of the Church
in the Internet
Age

Angela Ann Zukowski

CHAPTER 1

Sentinels
in Shifting Times

We are too mute in our faith. We need to change
passive Christians into active Christians.
—CARDINAL SUENENS

A quick survey of the cover stories in national and international magazines in the final decade of the twentieth century indicates a growing interest in spiritual and theological journeys. Stories and articles entitled "The Generation That Forgot God,"[1] "The Case of the Weeping Madonna,"[2] "The Pope's Plea,"[3] "The Rise of Christian Capitalists,"[4] "Solving the Mysteries of the Bible,"[5] "The Faith Factor,"[6] "And God Said . . ."[7] "Can We Still Believe in Miracles,"[8] "Is Jesus Really God?"[9] "God: What do you see?"[10] are some examples of the quest for spiritual meaning. If we add to these the many publications specializing in spirituality, the self-help guides to personal spiritual fulfillment, the increasing number of religious radio and TV programs, we find ourselves in an avalanche of diverse spiritual and religious ideas.

Finally, we cannot forget the rapid expansion of the Internet and the explosion of Web sites marketing their spiritual and theological ideas. The number of spiritual counselors and gurus is multiplying in cyberspace.[11] The Internet is frequently referred to as a new platform not only for believers but also for heretics. The religious and cultural landscape can be compared with a busy marketplace of ideas where competition thrives and seekers shop. If we wish to evaluate the spiritual stirrings as we cross the threshold into the new millennium, it is imperative that we study and be in tune with the developments in the new marketplace of culture and society.

In 1996 an article entitled "Finding God on the Web"[12] told the story of the Monastery of Christ in the Desert in northwestern New Mexico, which is plugged into the Internet (www.christdesert.org). The article tells how the monks use electricity generated by a dozen solar panels and a fragile data link through a single cellular phone to develop a heavily trafficked Benedictine home page and business. Neither can we forget the Diocese of Partenia (www.partenia.org)! This Web site of Bishop Gaillot opens the Church to thousands of people who are seeking new ways of "being church." In his book *The Soul of Cyberspace,* Jeff Zaleski reports that we really do not know how many more of these people are out there in cyberspace. "The Web is too big, too fluid, for an accurate account."[13] We know intuitively, and any surfer on the Web can confirm it, that we face a new and important phenomenon in this new territory or frontier called cyberspace. What does this new continent consist of? What influence will it continue to have? As evangelists responsible for proclaiming the Good News, what is our role, our mission in this new world?

Almost overnight the electronic community of the Internet has come to resemble a high-speed bazaar. This is where thousands of the faithful—and an equal number of the faithless—meet and debate and swap ideas about things that many of us have long since stopped discussing in public about our faith and religious beliefs. The interreligious conversation brings together Catholics, Protestants, Jews, Muslims, Buddhists and New Age seekers. In a *Time* article, Joshua Cooper Ramo writes "It is an astonishing act of technological and intellectual mainstreaming that is changing the character of the Internet, and could even change our minds about God."[14]

These are but a few indicators of an insatiable appetite for religion and spirituality that is boiling up within all cultures. There was a time when a spiritual journey meant a "dark night" of the soul, an internal exploration by way of retreats in silent getaway places such as monasteries, convents, or hermitages. Today the spiritual quest is positioned within a public forum in a new marketplace of prolific information and communication.

This revolution, and it is not a particularly "quiet" revolution, is in the process of modifying the religious and spiritual practices of men and women in every country and culture. In his book *Pilgrim Church,* William Bausch states that it would be almost superfluous to say that the Catholic Church is going through a time of confusion, crises, and turmoil resulting from the Information Age. The Church has been going through confusion, crises, and turmoil from the very beginning.[15] Yet, amid this cacophony of images, words, and sounds trumpeted by the new information the Church faces the challenge of a dialectical relationship between the demands and dangers of a situation in which she must find an identity without isolation and achieve relevance without abandoning what she believes.[16]

How does the Church evangelize within the new information landscape that is being woven into the cross-cultural fabric of religious and spiritual life? It is clear that we are witnessing a new realization of the sense of the sacred, of the Totally Other, of religious tradition, and of the spiritual life stirred up by this new age of communication and its environment. We also discover that individuals are being plunged into a spiritual malaise originating from their inability to relate their new religious experiences to the traditional concepts of Church teaching on what it means to be Christian. Furthermore, we cannot ignore the resurgence of a new conservatism, a new fundamentalism within the Church and society.

An informal research project conducted by the Institute for Pastoral Initiatives over three years indicates an interesting profile of people's attitudes toward the new media—particularly the Internet:

Generation.com (3–27)	28–40	41–60	61+
Very hot	Warm	Cool	Getting warm & growing hot

Members of Generation.com (ages 3–27) are totally at home in the new communications era. Since one or more computers may be found in their homes (due to parent's work and school requirements) computers and the Internet exist as an ordinary, not an exceptional, tool in their lives. There is no question about whether we should or shouldn't utilize the computer-related tools; the question is how we can expand their capabilities for greater access to the wide world of information and global networking.

The 28–40 group is warm toward the value of the computer and Internet in their lives. First, they are young enough to be part of the rapid explosion of the positioning of these communication resources within their workplace. The world is exploding in e-commerce. Most jobs in the marketplace require basic skills and understanding of computers and the Internet. Teachers are required to be literate in both of these to teach in any school today. The impact of the new Educational Technology Standards is shifting the paradigm of learning in our schools. Families in this age group are therefore directly impacted by the requirements that their children have to be computer/Internet literate. Thus, people in this segment are influenced by both work and education to be receptive to the new media culture.

Members of the 41–60 group tend to be cool to the new media. These communications technologies have not been part of the fabric of their lives. They are comfortable with the communication resources at hand and they see no reason to change. For many of them computers, and particularly the Internet, seem to be causing more confusion and chaos in people's lives than ever before. They perceive computers to be distracting, directing attention from interpersonal relationships, filling the mind with copious information that is not healthy for an individual and simply not necessary to life. Furthermore, they believe media, computers, and the Internet drain a family, school, or parish's budget that is already stretched too thin. There are, of course, exceptions to these generalizations. There are women and men in their forties and fifties who are as savvy as many generation.com'ers; however, this appears not to be the norm today. This group tends to be more cautious and reserved about the implementation of computers and the Internet into our ministries. Interestingly, many of the people in this age group who were surveyed are lay or clerical ecclesial leaders.

The most interesting is the 61+ group. They are not only getting warm but also growing hot, especially in regard to their Internet abilities. We are told they are the fastest group joining the navigational flow in cyberspace. Why? Well, we think it is quite clear. They are interested in communication with family and connectedness with the world. This is the very reason that some people in the next younger group (41–60) might resist the expansion of computers and the Internet in our lives; it is an attraction for this group. Thus, we find the 61+ group discovering new relationships and resources for keeping abreast of the world and cultural affairs. As computers grow in artificial intelligence and capability to assist in declining physical skills of older persons, the use of computers and the Internet could be a "saving grace" for dignity in growing older.

What is most significant about the above diagram is that as the years go by the ends of the continuum will meet in the center. As both ends continue to heat up—perceiving computers and the Internet to be as ordinary as the telephone is to all of us today—the questions about their place in our lives will evaporate. However, our concern with what is "available" via the Internet (information), its ease of accessibility, and its impact on our lives in the postmodern world will continue to escalate. Teaching our children new techniques for critical thinking and discernment amidst the plethora of information is a necessity. Furthermore, we wonder, how does the Church evangelize within the new information landscape?

The new media landscape acts as leaven in the daily bread of our lives. The community of faith needs to be alert to how believers and nonbelievers are being influenced and reshaped by the media landscape. This is especially important as more people spend a quantity of time in cyberspace. While our traditional means for communicating the faith remain valid, they are not exclusive. The Internet offers new or additional opportunities to image and position the Good News within a growing matrix of religious and spiritual realities in cyberspace.

In *Shopping for Faith,* Richard Cimino and Don Lattin predict that in the new millennium many young people and young adults, both Christians and Jews, will be returning to traditional congregations and their time-tested rituals, proving that the "spiritual supermarket" does not necessarily lead to wild religious experimentation.[17] They further predict that in the future, divisions between congregations favoring more traditional forms of ministry and those promoting contemporary worship may grow even more divisive. There is truly a cacophony of messages, experiences, and predictions not only within our local cultures but also within the global context.

——) **M**arketplace Trends Influencing Our Evangelization Efforts

When we look at the world, we realize that we are faced with a complex of postmodern trends and issues that will without a doubt exercise considerable influence on our efforts to evangelize. The new media landscape acts as a kind of yeast to their expansion and infiltration into all areas of our spiritual or religious lives.[18] We cannot ignore these. We need to consider the challenges ahead, asking about the direction of present trends and considering their impact on our future. We need to understand how communities, especially faith communities, are being reshaped by the diversity of these trends. This is imperative if we are to find an effective way to capture the religious imagination of the people by marketing, that is by imaging and positioning the Good News within a growing matrix of religious and spiritual realities.

An effective evangelization process requires that we recognize and name those realities that must be addressed and/or confronted if the Good News is to be communicated effectively in order to be heard, experienced, and embraced.

What are some of the cultural trends that need to be considered as we map our evangelization efforts for the new millennium? Let's consider a few that are critical to our immediate situation. These are: growing secularism, an eclipse of mystery, individualism, faith syncretism, spiritual seekers, fundamentalism, and emerging spiritual and religious realities in the new world.

Growing Secularism

In the new millennium, the separation of spirituality from religious institutions and congregations gives the modern spiritual quest a "free-floating" quality that can easily attach itself to a wide range of secular activities and social movements. Secularism is the outlook on life that reduces all value and meaning to the confines of this world.

Pope John Paul II, in *Tertio Millennio Adveniente (On the Coming of the Third Millennium)*, asks: "How can we remain silent, for example, about the religious indifference which causes many people today to live as if God did not exist, or to be content with a vague religiosity, incapable of coming to grips with the question of truth and the requirement of consistency?" (#36)

William Bausch indicates that secularism is characterized simultaneously by the loss of a vocabulary related to the supernatural and the loss of tradition. Secularism further expresses itself when sacred words, teachings, texts, symbols, and rituals are forgotten.[19] Secularism is characterized by relativism holding that truth does not exist in itself;

there are only historically conditioned statements that work in time-conditioned ways and places. There is a sense among some that secularism leads to a loss of transcendence while it embraces an integration of psychology and spirituality. Postmodern spirituality sees the spiritual as though it were embodied within the human body itself, nature, and society.

In 1985 the European bishops focused on these issues in depth:

> Underlying the bishops' concern is the awareness of an unprecedented and accelerating secularization: the family, the school, and the community appear increasingly unable to provide a context in which the faith can be learned and lived; religion is privatized and marginalized in society; religion is no longer considered a "natural" aspect of human life, but a rather eccentric personal opinion. In essence, this means that as people arrive at a personal synthesis of values at some stage in their lives, it is less likely that they will take as a central framework of ideals a belief in a transcendent God, Jesus Christ and the Gospel, or other traditional motivating symbols of the Christian community.[20]

The Rejection of Mystery

There seems to be a great refusal to believe in the presence of God. It appears our world suffers from an eclipse of mystery. James Bacik explains, "Mystery is what eludes rational control, which defies rational calculation and which exceeds all imagining. Mystery is that which sustains and draws us while remaining forever inexhaustible." Bacik goes on to indicate that for many in today's world, this Mystery is hidden, forgotten, distorted, or buried in some forgotten gravesite. The cause of this eclipse is perhaps secularism and consumerism that tends to exclude all forms of transcendence and religiosity in the dominant culture and from public and civic life.[21]

Individualism

Society in the developed world is becoming more fragmented, individualistic, and cut off from traditional forms of community. The emphasis on the individual is one reason for the growth in evangelical Christian denominations. The evangelical mindset focuses on personal change, personal spirituality, and personal salvation. Andrew Greeley argues that since the Second Vatican Council there is a dramatic emergence of "do-it-yourself" Catholicism in which believers pick and choose what they will believe and what teachings they will follow.[22] Peter Berger describes the doctrinal and existential dilemma faced by churches and believers in an age of competitive individualism and the dissolution of community—where religious affiliation is voluntary, every authority is questioned, and religious pluralism drifts easily toward indifference. Robert Ludwig suggests that an excessive individualism prevents people from seeing their interconnectedness and interdependence and hides the fact that individuals are embedded in social arrangements and in economic and political structures.[23]

Religious Syncretism

We have in the marketplace of religious thought a wide range of spiritual self-help books and media resources, which comprise an endless menu of spiritual teachings that can be selected and combined to suit individual needs. A person may be attracted to eastern spirituality, New Age spirituality, monastic spirituality, Catholicism, Lutheranism, or any combination of religious or spiritual beliefs or traditions. Rising interest in Eastern faiths like Buddhism, Taoism, Hinduism, and Sufism is part of the broader movement toward experiential spirituality.

The practice of Eastern forms of mysticism, such as meditation, does not require the same kind of loyalty to an exclusive belief system as Christianity or Islam often does. Robert Ludwig uses the image of a smorgasbord table of beliefs and practices of indigenous peoples and various New Age spiritual developments that fold into a "personalized" spirituality. Syncretism is due to the blending (mix and matching) of different faiths and also to declining religious loyalties. In today's marketplace of religion, fewer people feel pressured to stay within the confines of their religious heritage.

Spiritual Seekers

A growing discontent with institutional religion is leading a group of people known as "spiritual seekers" to navigate the religious landscape. These people have dropped out of—or had never become institutionally involved in—religious institutions despite a deep personal interest in spirituality. Spirituality and religious faith are increasingly viewed as individual, private matters with few connections to a congregation or faith community. There is an experiential spirituality that places primacy not on reason, not on belief systems, but rather on mystical experiences.

Harvey Cox sees this desire to experiment as a radical personal piety whereby seekers are comparing their own symbols and practices against what they learn as they experience life.[24] These people often consider themselves very "spiritual," but not very "religious."

These "spiritual seekers" may also turn to religious cults to feed their spiritual hunger. Sociologists say that those who tend to navigate in this direction are searching for family, belonging, and leadership. Increased isolation and lack of education seem to make individuals receptive to cultic religious groups in their longing for community.

As the entertainment media become the primary conveyer of common culture, spiritual seekers find them a haven for their journey. The media will continue to compete with religious groups as the main bearer of spiritual and religious insight, no matter how mundane and homogenized their revelations may be.[25] The end of the twentieth century, for example, manifests Hollywood's approach to nontraditional religious stories. Films such as *Contact, Ghost, Kundun, Seven Years in Tibet, Phenomenon* and others show this trend. According to a 1996 report by the Center for the Study of Social and Political Change, the film industry has veered away from traditional religious themes but continues to be fascinated by the spiritual and supernatural. The study analyzed the content of hundreds of popular films produced from 1946 to 1990 and found that favorable portrayal of traditional religious characters and institutions declined with each decade. As traditional religious themes waned, there were increasing depictions of alternative sources of spirituality.

We cannot forget the influence of music. Music—especially New Age music—contributes to the spiritual and religious evolution, mesmerizing the spiritual seekers and subduing them on their journey. Music pulses with secular spirituality. We find that instead of urging people to go back to church, or to pray, the message is resolutely iconoclastic. The songs seem to say that in a godless society the only recourse is to make a personal appeal to the divine. Popular culture generates its own religious icons while soothing the seekers with a terrestrial hum and, often, subliminal messages.

To aid the spiritual seekers there is a revival of interest in angels. An article in *Life* magazine about angels indicates that "angel" Web sites have surfaced on the Internet, three glossy American magazines devoted exclusively to angels recently appeared, and hundreds of new nonfiction books about angels continue to appear in our bookstores.

We should not forget angel jewelry and other forms of secular art—angel bears, angel penguins, and angel birds. The debate about popular culture pits those who complain that popular culture vulgarizes and trivializes spirituality, marketing it to satisfy consumer tastes, against those like Phyllis Tickle, who believes that popular media "democratize theology" by bringing God-talk into everyday life.[26]

Fundamentalism

Fundamentalism is a distinct set of beliefs and practices. It is a language, a discursive style, a way of talking, of communicating something important to one's self and to one's fellow believers about the sacred, about how to live, and even about how to act out one's values in broader social settings.[27] The fundamentalist movement arose in an atmosphere of intellectual and theological debate between conservatives and liberals.

David Tracy sees fundamentalism as a first reaction against modernity. He indicates that it has a wide spectrum covering areas "from the Islamic fundamentalism of Ayatollah Khomeini's movement to the Roman Catholic traditionalism of Archbishop Lefebevre's movement; from Rabbi Kehan's rereading of Judaism to the emergent Hindu fundamentalism in India and Shinto fundamentalism in Japan, and several new religious cults." Tracy waves the warning flag for us. He indicates that what we least expected has happened: "a resurgence of antimodern, antiliberal, antiprivatized, aggressive religious movements across the globe."[28] This is part of the religious panorama with which we must contend.

At the heart of Christian fundamentalism is the emphasis on inerrancy, or the literal truth of Scripture. It is a theological interpretation of the Christian faith whose mainspring is that the Bible is without error in everything it asserts. This is its most attractive feature.

One of the characteristics of fundamentalism is the intensity with which fundamentalists hold their beliefs. They generally refuse to acknowledge the existence of any religious perspectives outside of their own. Fundamentalist apologetics constructs a system, which holds that since God has revealed himself in a book that is without error, he is to be found uniquely within the pages of that book. Edgar Towne believes that this characteristic of fundamentalism is a kind of idolatry that replaces Christ with the Bible. (Other religious traditions might use a different book in the same way as the authority that guides the Church or religious tradition.) In this regard the challenge of fundamentalism to the Church is theological and spiritual.[29] Fundamentalism offers the mainline churches a challenging opportunity to rethink their theory of mission and the way in which they present themselves in public. Without a doubt, fundamentalism poses a theological challenge to mainline churches.

It is not surprising to discover that "the fundamentalist upheavals that have shaken large parts of the world have found an echo in the growth of the electronic church."[30] The evangelists of the electronic church found out very early that their worldview is shared by a great number of cultures. A great number of people receive their transmissions around the world. We can say that, in a number of countries and in multiple cultures, they are gathering a public that is countercultural. This counterculture opposes the liberal or laissez-faire attitude not only in society but also in culture and government.

The electronic church with its prominent television ministries expresses a fairly stable, coherent, and conservative worldview that serves more to rally believers than to recruit or convert others. Gallup research shows that the viewers of the electronic church are older, in a lower income and educational bracket, and more "fundamentalist" in their attitudes than those who do not watch. This practice does not mean that they do not attend church, but perhaps it is seen to complement what they find there.

The message of the electronic church is comforting for some and provoking to others. There is virtually no home in the world that has access to radio, television, cable TV, Web TV, or the Internet to which the electronic church cannot send its songs, its sermons, and its appeals for contributions. It has brought to millions of people all over the world a new way of experiencing religion. The electronic church's success reflects the cultural drift (some would say stampede) toward conservatism. Whatever else we may think of them, the electronic evangelists have propelled the church into the electronic age. Their aggressive use of television, communication satellites, the Internet, and mass marketing techniques has implications that the Church is only beginning to grapple with.

The development of the electronic church, the predominant role it plays among the evangelists, and the reasons for its phenomenal success are to be seen as part of the revolution in electronic communications. Neither the technology nor the ways it is being used are unique to the electronic church. Rather it is the church's intense use of the medium to propagate the message to a number of cultures around the world. If the danger of the electronic media is to favor passive consumption, then electronic religion can easily become a religion of push-button spiritual gratification, mere appearance, and instant release—one that bypasses a real, personal commitment lived out in everyday life, physical and social contact with other believers, and involvement in a local church community with outreach to others. We cannot forget that Christian fundamentalism foments an exclusionist and escapist mentality.

Emerging Global Religious and Spiritual Realities

We cannot ignore the observation of the futurists who study the growing influence, more and more apparent, that religion and spirituality exercise on the evolution of society, politics, culture, and the media. They may give us clues about how we are to evangelize: to whom, when, why, where, and how we are to engage in evangelization and marketing the Gospel. We see a growing reaffirmation of religious identity in Eastern and Central Europe. After seven decades of being denied religious freedom, many residents of these countries are hungry for spirituality. We have already seen battles between religious groups from outside the area who want to proselytize and the traditional religions, Sunni Islam in Uzbekistan, Catholicism in Poland, the Orthodox Church in Russia, who want to return to traditional forms of worship.

Latin America continues to be a theater of expansion for the evangelical church, particularly the Pentecostal churches. Numerous

Islamic factions are tearing apart the Middle East, the domain of Islam, each with its own objective. African countries continue to see the struggle between Islam and Christianity while traditional African religions try to position themselves in the marketplace. China will continue to engage in the challenges that underground religion presents to it. At the same time, the infusion of Christianity in emerging countries of Asia such as Thailand, South Korea, and Taiwan is remarkable. Projections indicate that growth in these countries will continue.[31] We also know that the conflict between the Arabs and the Jews is not simply a dispute over territory. Great misunderstandings deeply rooted in religious and ethnic conflict, which has evolved for thousands of years, complicate it.

This new landscape that we have described constitutes a major challenge for the Church. As the Church sees the flowering of these new cultic spiritual and religious searchers, the questions posed by Paul VI in *Evangelii Nuntiandi* are especially pertinent for today.

> In our day, what has happened today to the hidden energy of the Good News, which is able to have a powerful effect on man's conscience?
>
> To what extent and in what way is that evangelical force capable of really transforming the people of this century?
>
> What methods should be followed in order that the power of the Gospel may have its effect? (#4)

—) **A** Compelling Religious Imagination

The trends that we have discovered indicate momentous changes in the process that oblige us to radically review the manner in which we understand the traditional Church, in particular the role of the Gospel and where it belongs in this new world. As we enter the third millennium and its new cultural context, there must be a new evangelization depending in large measure on the choices the Church makes in facing the challenges of contemporary culture.

Michael Warren states "part of the problem of the Church in our time is offering a compelling religious imagination of life in the face of other agencies offering attractive alternatives."[32] It is an important perspective for writing this book. How are we going to capture the religious imagination not only of the "spiritual seekers, the unconverted, the nominally converted practicing and not practicing people as well as the dedicated active people for whom an authentically lived, witnessing faith makes a difference in their lives, their families, parish and local cultures?"

We can approach the new landscape we are addressing here in several ways. We can engage it either with resistance or with a dialogical approach. These approaches are not meant to be exclusive of one another or any others. They are points of contact for conversation and action.

Warren indicates, "If the Church wants to be a zone of influence, it could be one only by examining carefully and thinking wisely about these other influences."[33] He presents us with compelling ideas that the Church can exist as a zone of significance "offering an imagination of life it claims is not only worthy [of] following but is salvific liberating us for a new kind of life."[34] The processes we design will be conditioned by the cultural context and the lived experience of the local faith community.

There are some who may encourage us simply to engage in a cultural resistance approach. There is no doubt that resistance may be the most direct and uncomplicated route to assume. This does not mean that it would not leave scars and/or ultimately death, as the history of the church shows. Yet, resistance can be a profound safeguard for the faith. While it may lead to a Diaspora religious situation—which may be inevitable anyway—it does create the boundaries from within which individuals can encounter an authentic traditional living community. A profound sense of religious or Catholic identity can emerge and be nurtured here. Yet, how do an incarnational or trinitarian theology and spirituality relate to a resistance theory or approach?

Lest we leave our readers with the impression that we are against cultural resistance, we are not. We are only seeking to define the balance. Pope John Paul II in speaking to the Catholic educators in Canada in 1984 said: "The radically different cultural expressions and activities of our times, especially those which catch the popular attention of young people, demand that educators be open to new cultural influences and be capable of interpreting them for young people in the light of the Christian faith and of Christ's universal command of love." There is a tension between the Church and culture that is amplified by the media. Pope John Paul II in many of his speeches demands that the Church could be a system of significance within contemporary culture. Warren states that "the maintaining of a religious signifying system is more intentional and demands more energy than that of the wider culture, partly because the significance of religious realities are not as obvious, not as 'material.'"[35]

Bernard Haring believes that a dialogical approach to culture is one way of coming to terms with the cultural tension. He begins by stating that one needs to have a good grip on understanding our Catholic identity and mission if the dialogue is to be effective. This presupposes that there is a living faith community that perceives that the Church is not only a prophetic voice but is willing to listen and share in the joys and hopes, the anguish and fears of all people. Haring reminds us that communication in the church and through the Church is for the sake of community, for the unity of humankind. But communication or evangelization does not automatically bring about community. There is need for dialogue, for conversation, for being with and for each other.[36]

To the Greeks *dialogos* meant a free flow of meaning through a group. This allows the group to discover insights not individually attainable. Dialogue demands concern and hospitality toward the other, as well as respectful acceptance of the other's identity, modes of expression, and values. Dialogue requires authentic listening to one another. Dialogue opens doors and creative ways for the Holy Spirit to "stir the hearts."

In *The Courage to Teach,* Parker Palmer explores the importance of dialogue for ministry. He says that we need "ground rules for dialogue that allow us to be present to another person's problems in a quiet, receptive way that encourages the soul to come forth, a way that does not presume to know what is right for the other but allows the other's soul to find its own answers at its own level and pace."[37] All too often in ministry we are too ready to give an answer without first opening the space for the other person to reveal him- or herself. Respecting the inner journey, the questions and fears associated with that journey, as an individual seeks to know his or her own identity is key to the dialogical process. However, for this approach to be effective, ministers must have a sense of identity and integrity. They need to know who they are and what they are called to be and become. Confidence in their mission and vision enables the minister to create what Palmer calls "communities of discourse." There must be space where individuals can honestly be themselves as they explore the great and fundamental questions about the meaning of life, the All Holy, the Transcendent—God. It is here, in such a space, that authentic dialogue can occur.

Those who desire to be communicators of the Gospel need to be aware that effective dialogue requires attentive listening. *Communio et Progressio (Pastoral Instruction on Social Communication)* states: "A teaching Church that is not, above all, a learning, listening Church is not on the wavelength of divine communication" (#175). Thus, if our evangelization efforts are to bring about change, evangelizers must realize that in the process of dialogue information is not only going forth but also is flowing back in such a way that the evangelizers—the Church—learn and are changed.

—) The Image and Position of the Church in the New Religious Panorama

When we speak of a new way to present the image of the Church or the Good News, we are speaking the language of marketing. We have to keep in mind that it is the institution's image, not necessarily its reality (essence), that people initially respond to. Therefore, witness, dialogue and positioning, even resistance, are critical to how the message is delivered and received by the receiver. The cacophony of spiritual and religious profiles we addressed earlier requires that the Church constantly seek ways to create a more positive image in the minds of both members and nonmembers among the multiplicity of images in the new marketplace.

What is the meaning of *image?* An image is the sum of feelings, beliefs, attitudes, impressions, thoughts, perception, ideas, recollections, conclusions, and mindsets that a person or group has of another person, organization, or object. Its image is a function of its deeds and its communications. It not for us to hide the good deeds of the "lived Gospel values" under the bushel basket, but to put it on the mountaintop for all to see! "You are the light of the world. A city built on a hill cannot be hid. No one after lighting a lamp puts it under a bushel basket, but on the lampstand, and it gives light to all the house. In the same way, let your light shine before others, so that they may see your good works and give glory to your Father in heaven" (Matthew 5:14–16).

Could it be that we can find the principle to guide us in conceptualizing the image of the Good News today in the Gospel of Matthew? What are the lampstands or mountaintops of contemporary culture? As catechists and evangelizers of the Good News, we see the new media landscape and especially the Internet as the contemporary lampstand and mountaintop, offering us new opportunities to not only lift the light from under the basket but also to set up reflectors behind the light to expand and intensify the light of the Good News!

——) Conclusion

Evangelii Nuntiandi states, "For the Church, evangelization means bringing the Good News into all strata of humanity, and through its influence, transforming humanity from within and making it new" (#18). The movement of "bringing the Good News into all strata of humanity" demands that we understand "all" the bases where humanity communicates with one another. This calls for a radical paradigm shift from our traditional understanding of how and where we communicate the Good News. We encourage the Church leaders and ministers to avoid the so-called "tyranny of either/or." This means we cannot root ourselves in only one means of communication to proclaim the Good News to transform humanity while ignoring the others as irrelevant. We must use all the means and processes of communication directly or indirectly related to humanity. This is particularly imperative as the new media landscape and Internet continue to be woven into the ordinary tapestry of people's lives.

In an interview Cardinal Suenens spoke about the need for a "New Pentecost" in the Church. He states, "We are too mute in our faith. We need to change passive Christians into active Christians."[38] We must realize that today differs from the past. It is one thing to Christianize the culture of a tribe, where there is only one set of cultural traits and life is relatively simple. It is quite another to influence a society that contains many subcultures and a vast array of media messages bombarding the senses and attempting to capture the spiritual imagination of the people. The evangelization of the twenty-first century is a challenge not to do things differently but to do different things.

We already feel a tingling of something new happening around us, as indicated in this chapter. It is like tremors we feel and see demonstrated on a seismograph. We cannot claim ignorance and close our eyes to the new reality boiling up around us. If we sense that what is happening around us does not quite fit our traditional understandings and interpretations of faith, religion, or spirituality, we should not turn our backs on the experiences and events. We must confront them head on. We must come to terms with the fact that a new place—cyberspace—has been found. This "new place" is a new frontier. It is a new culture being formed with or without us. Therefore we must constantly ask ourselves, what is this new place? How is this new place being packaged or marketed? What is going on in this new place? What is the meaning of the spiritual and religious messages that are swirling through the new places? Is there something we can learn from our observations? Is there here an invitation to consider a shifting of our paradigm for communicating the Good News?

Edward Schillebeeckx's vision of how the Church is to engage in the shifting religious landscape is quite clear. He indicates that if we analyze the various Synoptic, Pauline, Johannine, and Petrine traditions in the New Testament, we find within the same cultural period Christians expressing that faith within divergent paradigms and models. He believes that striving for one and the same paradigm throughout the word would lead to an impoverishment of the Gospel's very message. The Gospel's message is too rich to be contained within one paradigm.[39] If we believe that the Spirit of the Lord calls every person and each culture to its own fresh and creative response to the Gospel, perhaps we need to shake off the sluggishness of time past and allow our lives to be reawakened with a "New Pentecost" as recommended by Cardinal Suenens. Yes, we need to shift our paradigm for communicating the Gospel within the new landscapes that are blossoming around us. We are living in a *kairos* moment of history. This moment calls for us to engage in a new evangelization. What is it we are called to do? How are we to do it?

——) **Q**uestions for Reflection

1. How would you describe the new religious panorama within which we are living?

2. How do you respond to the cultural trends identified in this chapter? Are there others you feel are relevant to our discussion?

3. How would you evaluate the Church's, or your parish or school's, use of the new media culture for evangelization and catechesis? Do you think the Internet is a place worth considering for evangelization and catechesis?

4. What has been your experience with the Internet for gathering information about religion or spirituality?

5. How can the Church more effectively communicate and be in dialogue via the Internet?

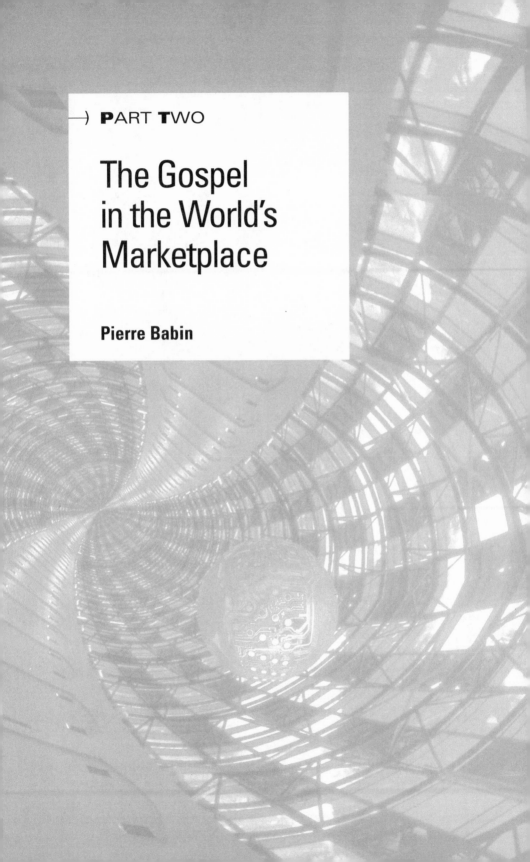

→ **P**ART **T**WO

The Gospel
in the World's
Marketplace

Pierre Babin

CHAPTER 2

The Star System and the Gospel

Evangelization according to Christ means primarily that
the evangelizer has personally felt the great
movements, the basic questions, the
rebellions, and the aspirations
of the time.

⟶ Let Us Climb Up to the Areopagus

I have always been attracted to the story of Paul the Apostle strolling through the streets of Athens and being filled with wonder at the many temples and shrines that the Greek people used in their daily worship. He then climbed to the Areopagus, where the Greek thinkers and philosophers debated their beliefs. There Paul spoke of Christ and met with limited success. What audacity! What rhetoric! (Acts 17:16–32).

In his recent encyclical *Remptoris Missio (On Missionary Activity)*, Pope John Paul II uses this visual and symbolic example from Paul's life. Here the pope invites Christians to adopt an attitude similar to Paul's for our own day in which the media and technologies are making a new culture. "The most important Areopagus of modern time is the world of communications. . . . It is not enough to utilize the media to spread the Christian message. . . . It is also necessary to integrate this message into the "new culture" created by modern methods of communication (#37).

In the following pages I will be trying to climb to the Areopagus of modern times and to be in dialogue with the new media culture. It is a difficult task that will most often satisfy no one. This was the same for Paul in his own time. When he spoke in Athens he shook up the wise but made few disciples. Nonetheless he created inroads that marked all of Christianity through the centuries.

May the reflections that follow enrich our dialogue as faithfully as Paul's!

—) **W**hat Is the Relationship Between Stardom, Success, and the Gospel?

One of the fundamental categories I find immediately in the world of the media is the desire for success. This success is linked to the audience and consequently to publicity and money. Americans, more immersed than the French in media culture, always surprise me by asking me right away: "Are you successful?" Coming from a literary culture where precise, even humble ideas have primacy, I was at first almost scandalized.

The second category, twin to success, is the star system. This brings to mind the film *Jesus Christ Superstar.* Would Jesus have cultivated success? Can he be considered a celebrity? As Christians, should we seek success, should we join the race to find an audience, to seek stardom? Fr. Antonio Ergo, in charge of religious programs on Portuguese TV, told me, "When I first produced programs on TV, I dedicated all my time to creating, to making good images. Now that I am responsible for prime-time TV programs, I spend my time in reading the audience surveys."

Is this a good idea? In spite of my reluctance, working through these topics I have recognized that there is some harmony between the Gospels and the media categories of stardom and success.

What is the relationship between success and the Gospel? The first answer to that question can be found in a dictionary. After recalling the etymology of the word "success" (Latin, *successes,* verb, *succedere,* to proceed under), Robert's French dictionary gives this first definition: "Whatever good or bad follows an action, an initial fact." Though subsequently the word might have been used mostly to mean positive outcome and good result, I take it here in its first fundamental meaning: what is essential to success is not the (successful in the modern sense of the term) outcome but the impact.

Therefore how can we deny that Jesus was a success? His person and his actions had tremendous results in his lifetime and still more after his death. The Bible, including the Gospels, remains the best selling book in the world. We can say that the success of the Gospel is intrinsically tied to its impact. This is not a pleasant doctrine, but it is an event with impact. The day it ceases to have an impact, the Gospel stops as well.

We can imagine Jesus taking a bus to go from downtown to the suburbs of large cities like Paris, New York, London, Calcutta, or São Paulo. He is lost in these "supercities" of 20 to 50 million inhabitants, which, unless a catastrophe happens, will be characteristic of living conditions in the future.[1]

Jesus is pushing his shopping cart in a huge shopping center. Jesus is in the suburbs, among the wealthy and the downtrodden, the outcasts and those under police protection. Jesus is among the unemployed and senior citizens, among the young wearing wild hairdos. What would Jesus say? What would he do? Would he weep for our cities as he did for Jerusalem? One thing can be considered certain: he would succeed in having an impact. As before, he would raise enthusiasm and conflict. Why?

⟶) Proclaiming the Gospel Means Continuing Its Impact

We should not identify Jesus with the media. Jesus was not a journalist. He did not narrate events, he created them. The first journalists, as one could call Peter, and Paul, and the evangelists, only reflect the impact of Jesus. Comparatively, the Gospel is an event of Jesus himself. Yet both journalists and evangelists have this in common: they look primarily to the impact, whether it is called a scoop or a miracle. They are concerned with the number of issues sold or the number of the faithful gathered.

Jesus, like a journalist, inserts himself into the very fabric of the misfortunes and drama of life. He sees the sick and the sinners rather than the healthy, derailed trains rather than those that arrive on schedule. The Good News is not a proclamation from a heaven beyond time; it is a strike against the diseases and exploitation of people of Jesus' time.

What was Jesus' secret? He displayed a love and a vision from elsewhere. From the time he ran away to the Temple in Jerusalem when he was twelve years old, Jesus showed an uncommon character and discernment. By running away in this manner and at such a young age Jesus showed an awareness that evil was already a painful experience. This is whether the evil is called Satan, paralysis or neurosis, the domination of the rich, or the hypocrisies of the priests. Jesus knew it. Moreover, living in close relationship with his Father, Jesus showed an incredible power, not only to attract people, but also to help them solve their problems. The secret of his impact is the same thing we find in all of the great movies. Jesus knew the evil of his generation. Jesus incarnated the great cosmic fight between Good and Evil. In the end evil is washed away by the influence of the Gospel.

It is up to us, as little prophets, not to simply repeat the timeless good news, but to hear the cries of our people, beginning with those who are most in need. At the same time it is to harmonize misfortune and happiness, hardships and Good News. Knowing how to express the Gospel on TV is a secondary, if not mistaken, strategy. The real question is this: how can we make an impact? How can we, by speaking the language of our own people, become involved in the great struggle between slavery and freedom, between disease and life, between death and the fullness of life? Success in Christian terms is this type of impact. We now must analyze this more closely for we touch here one of the fundamental questions asked everyday to all Christian communicators.

—) **S**uccess as Seen by a Christian

If a Christian can speak of success without feeling reluctant, it is because Jesus gives the word success dimensions that cannot be found in Hollywood. These are

> total trust in the Father,
> having an impact on the acute pains of the world,
> the cross.

Doubtless Jesus had the exceptional psychic gifts to heal and to multiply loaves. These abilities are not specific to "Christian success." What is specifically Christian is Jesus' total trust in the One he called Father. Jesus said these incredible words immediately before Lazarus' resurrection, "Father, I thank you for having heard me. I knew that you always hear me" (John 11:41–42). He who can speak so is very powerful indeed; the source of life flows through him freely.

Another cause of success is that the Messiah is the one who touches directly the misery of the people. He goes straight to where it hurts, where the evil is. He drives the demons of his time out in concrete and radical ways. He makes people stand up, he makes them see, he reintegrates them into the community and denounces the oppression of the religious authorities.

Ultimately Christian success has an original character; it involves the cross. The success of the "Christian star" is the way of the cross. There is no Christian success without going through the cross, the secret cross of agony and doubt, the cross of criticism and failure, the cross of desertion of friends, the cross of injustice and prison.

Why is the cross necessary? It is through the cross that we can achieve the death of the ego. The cross shows God's justice and strength to everyone. When the spectators saw Jesus fallen down and crucified, they understood what he meant even better than they did having seen all of his miraculous healing. "Certainly this man was innocent," said the centurion when Jesus died (Luke 23:47).

Jacques Séguéla, publicity agent who directed French President François Mitterand's election campaign, diagnosed it rightly. Politicians are aware of the importance of the media for massaging their ego. "Politics is sick from too many words, of too much false-ness. There are too many sentences, too much bombast, intoxicated by its own importance. It has lost its content. To exist is simple, it is enough to express one's soul, not one's ego."[2] In politics, it is not God's power that speaks, but the inflated little ego. Therefore politi-cians are not seeking the public good for anyone but themselves. Politicians hide too often behind beautiful rhetoric; it is the star in search of self, decorated in beautiful but empty sentimental words. Suffering is necessary to free us every day from the evil that never dies, namely the attachment to our ego. St. Paul understood it when after the wisdom of the speech at the Aeropagus of Athens, he decided to speak foolishly in Corinth. "For I decided to know nothing among you except Jesus Christ, and him crucified" (1 Corinthians 2:2).

In contrast to a worldly "movie star," Christ never sought his own glory. If there is a point where as a communicator I can measure my distance from Christ, it is there. I seek my own glory and my success sticks to me. Therefore the cross is as necessary for me as light, not so much because the cross strengthens by causing pain, but more because it kills my ego by making me lose face. The man Jesus hanging from the cross has lost the beautiful face of a "superstar." He no longer appeals to the crowds. He is forced to put himself into the hands of those who kill him. The cross is the loss of the beautiful picture. It is a mystery about which we do not know how to speak. We have to understand that for us as communicators the cross is not simply an optional way, a virtuous disposition of some kind; it is a necessity. We have to acknowledge criticism and exclusion, anguish and persecution, as a functional necessity. Just as it is necessary for cyclists competing in the Tour de France bicycle race to practice all year long for the test of the race, so it is necessary for evangelizers to put the test of the cross in their lives and practice it. They have to do this not to strengthen their muscles, but to empty themselves of ego. More than ever in this culture of the success brought about by the media, we are forced, in order to evangelize, to rejoice in our weaknesses. Like Paul, we must learn to say "Therefore I am content with weaknesses, insults, hardships, persecutions, and calamities for the sake of Christ; for whenever I am weak, then I am strong" (2 Corinthians 12:10).

In my opinion, if—for many Church people—the practice of the media is dangerous, it is because they bring to that ministry only the attitude of becoming a star, the expectation of personal glory and a misplaced vanity. They refuse to follow the way of the cross. This ministry should be entrusted only to those who have decided to embrace the cross.

Christians know the expression "when then ego gives up, God's power appears." Should we therefore seek weakness, hardship, and defeat? We should not look for suffering that can be avoided. I think that our communication should be rooted in a twofold attitude: success and flight, immersion in media and solitude. Christ in his public life shows that twofold aspect; he is immersed in the success of the multiplication of loaves, and in the evening he withdraws by himself on the mountain (John 6:1–15). It is dangerous to calculate the audience and to be elected by the public in a popularity contest. Therefore the solitude of being present to God and to one's self belongs to our daily discipline. What belongs specifically to the Christian success is neither loving the cross as such, nor downgrading one's self and being the lowest of all. It is the conviction that the cross is full of life and is the manifestation of God. Without the cross we are unable to relativize our ego and without it people cannot see what animates us from within.

The poor or suffering churches remind us better than any other example the meaning of the law of the cross. The magazine *Asia Focus* quotes the following words from a paper in Pakistan: "Contrary to the places where theology is built up in universities and relatively comfortable seminaries . . . the Church of Asia speaks more of the cross, of the weakness and *kenosis* [the Greek word for emptying one's self] of Jesus. Christians welcome more willingly a Church that is humble, patient, powerless, but living in hope."[3]

⟩ **T**he Success Option

The best prayer I know to guide and accompany a communicator in the battle to kill the ego is that from Baudelaire:

> Blessed are you, my God, who gives suffering
> As a divine remedy to our impurities,
> And the best and purest essence,
> That prepare the strong for the holy pleasures.[4]

The poet makes suffering "the best and purist essence" in the alchemic sense of "spirit," essential oil. And here is the point: suffering prepares and builds up strong believers just as the alchemist is said to change common matter into gold.

I think that in this New Age *(Aetatis Novae)*, the Church needs strong believers, communicators who are not afraid of the cross. The

Church has too many analysts, not enough creative people, and too many members who give repetitive answers, not enough who dare. If some Christians speak of the media and its success with so much mistrust, is it not because they are afraid to suffer and to shine the light of Christ? This was not the attitude of the apostles: all through the Acts of the Apostles we can see their audacity and their confidence.

If you are not able to take criticism, to face critics in the marketplace, if you don't dare to say "I," then you are not the person to be in charge of communication. To those who want to proclaim the Gospel in this new pluralistic and violent culture I would like to say, seek to make an impact, cultivate the kind of success that comes from total trust in God, from accepting the way of the cross and from a direct struggle against the great human troubles.

—) Troubles and Hopes

As we have said, success for the evangelist depends on making an impact on the sufferings and troubles of today's society. What has the human heart become under the influence of modern communications? Which messiah do the young generations become enthusiastic about, the cyborg killer played by Arnold Schwarzenegger in *The Terminator,* with Techno and Rap? To the groups coming to Taizé, the monastic community in France, the brothers used to say, "We have no answers, we are here to share your questions." Which questions?

I won't speak here of the problems inherent to the human condition such as becoming old, sick, suffering from inequality of opportunities due to situation and talents and so on. In the framework of this book, I am referring to "bad news," the troubles specific to this developing electronic civilization. May you uncover these things according to the Spirit dwelling within! The following reflections and proposals aim at stimulating your imagination.

I see two major risks, even two major troubles, belonging to the electronic culture. These are the loss of one's self and the exclusion from the world marketplace. Behind these obstacles there are two immense hopes: to be recognized for one's own originality and to cooperate with the hope that these technologies generate, namely, the unity of the world through diversity.

Losing One's Self

The loss of one's self comes from two major causes. On the one hand there is the illogical and emotional violence of media language. On the other, there is the crumbling of borders.

The first effect of the world of the media and the new electronic technologies is a kind of cultural earthquake. The walls protecting the human person that have been built up across the centuries in rural and industrial civilizations are falling into dust. In the turmoil of emotion and the glut of information the human being is slowly deprived of structure and becoming increasingly fragmented. Under the unconscious influence of magazines and TV programs people are losing the logical links of ideas and facts. Fictional stories and glossy production values are replacing reason. The firm foundations of tradition and teaching are falling down, being replaced by sound and visual modulations. Living is simply living "in the moment." When I asked a woman who was suffering "what is your sense of life, your reason for living?" there was no answer. Instead she answered, "If I find someone or something that fascinates me, that is my reason for living." So it appears that the demand for intellectual coherence must make room for the demand of psychic intensity.

For many young people vibrating in the currents of fashion, jumping from using their imagination to viewing the next video clip, dancing and surfing the Internet are their reason for living and its meaning. A taxi driver navigating Vienna's traffic jams once summed it up in the language of today: "With the life we live, we lose our inner being." Young people do not have a soul any more; they are only part of the traffic. In the evenings they watch detective stories or televised games, drugging themselves against being lost in life's traffic jams.

For many adults, the loss of direction is caused mostly by frantic economic development and the deregulation of their social image. One wants to be in the trend and noticed at any cost if possible. The advertising industry becomes the norm. In Tokyo, after an attack in the subway by members of the Aum sect, the auxiliary bishop, Paul Kazuhiro Mori, wrote, "By stressing the economic development, we have lost our deeper 'I.' Those who leave their home and join the Aum religion are sincere in their search for some spiritual experience. . . .

In a consumer society where money is everything, we have lost the sense of the inner world of the heart, which can be neither reached nor bought by the power or money."[5]

Remembering the words of the Gospel "Woe to the world because of stumbling blocks!" (Matthew 18:7), we can think today that scandal comes from a media environment that orients people outside themselves. In this society, we can fear that many children are not even open to the awakening of their innermost "I." They are being told, "Don't wear that!" "Look at all we've done for you." "If you want to succeed in life, you need good grades" and so on.

It is helpful for us to watch with teens the American stories showing what it means to live as a young person today. Seeing these stories we can understand that the "mortal sin" of this culture is not sex or violence, but conformity to the trends and habits of this world. You exist if you buy, if you do like the others, if you become the music with a headset stuck to your ears. Doing like others, obeying the laws of the world of adults and of money, resonating with the latest commercial, all are stifling any inner voice. This violence of modulation, this rumbling of the ads, prevents the emergence of that small voice coming from "a sound of sheer silence" (1 Kings 19:12). As I was interviewing Marcel Légaut on education, asking how he would advise educators of youth, he answered bluntly "Keep them away from adults." Adults represent for him the maximum of conformity, of a life deprived of one's self as a center.[6]

Another major cause of the loss of one's self is the disappearance of borders between countries leaving a sense of being uprooted. The "global village," "the planetary village," "worldwide application," all these phrases with their various nuances express one simple fact: electronics are changing the old categories of time and space. The old borders that sheltered human identity across the centuries are crumbling, allowing the emergence of the human being. Instead of these borders we have the Internet and cyberspace. What kind of people are we becoming when we, as Abraham did, lose the things that keep our lives rooted? Like Abraham we are losing the earth (leave your country), the social bonds that identify us (your kinship, your clan), the cultural traditions that support us (your father's house) (see Genesis 12:1).

Like Abraham, we can say that the electronic era is bringing us to transcend the traditional roots by which we defined ourselves according to where we lived, who our family was, and what society we belonged to. Today's drama revolves around the adults who are not prepared to make such a transformation. The young are without a doubt better prepared to make this transformation thanks to their travels and their "Internet mind." But what training have they received to help them define themselves from within? "Young people without borders" yes, but what have we built to replace these borders? Are we not still living in our countries just as medieval people lived in their castles?

For years we have linked language and religion in an intimate way with the emergence of the "I." We have taught people to live in particular cultures without relativizing them in terms of their foundational principles. In countries plagued by ethnic struggles, like Burundi and Rwanda, evangelization was tightly linked to cultural and social ways of thinking, no matter what the Church authorities say. We witness this as we watch their colorful liturgies, processions, dances, and orchestras. While such strategies worked for a while, that form of evangelization, happily rooted in the culture, is not sufficient for today's needs. The spiritual awakening of the individual, the emergence of a personal sense of vocation and of a personal inner guidance by the Spirit, has reached too few. Such guidance must be offered to the whole population, starting with the young. I do not see any other way to respond to the ethnic wars than the long work of awakening the inner being of each person. When we are enlightened in depth by a spiritual birth, by the experience of the inner "I," we no longer have to be reduced to simply belonging to a family, a nation or a religion.

How can we define that fundamental experience of the inner "I"? How can we define what C. G. Jung calls the "self"? In this work, why should we speak of losing the "self" rather than losing one's soul? I prefer to use a language closer to the human sciences, less marked by idealistic interpretations. The term "soul" implies for many people the idea of an entity distinct from the body, even in opposition to it: somehow the soul would be to the body what a facilitator is to a group. This is a notion unacceptable at the biblical level as well as for the media. I propose here the term of one's "self," which seems best to fit modern experience as well as that of biblical thought. Many people have recently spoken of that intimate experience of finding ourselves as personal beings emerging above the emotions, the flood of information and advertisements of today.

Whether we speak of soul, spirit, the "self," or "the depth of being" (Marcel Légaut), the "center of being" (G. Durckheim), the "bottom of the bottom of ourselves" (Goettmann), or the meaning (M. De Smedt), we find the same basic components:

- It is a reality that transcends us. Though it belongs to us, it transcends us. The terms normally used are "source," "mystery," "base," "depth of being," "beyond."

- It is a reality that we own, that comes from us, that is not conferred on us by some external teaching. It is the same as breathing.

- It is an experiential reality. It is felt, it is experienced, it can be described in metaphorical terms. Ultimately it is a reality providing an immovable foundation, a stability in the emotional turmoils and stresses in life.

Behind these terms used above, we can refer to the definition of C. G. Jung: "The Self is a psychic reality, made of consciousness and of the infinite ocean in which it floats. My soul and my consciousness here is my 'self' in which I am enveloped like an island on the sea, like a star in the sky. So the 'self' is infinitely more vast than the 'ego.'"[7]

In the recent wars between races and religions, the increase in terrorism leads us to understand that we have defined ourselves too much by country, religion, or race. We see ourselves primarily as American or French or Indian, Tutsi or Hutu, and only secondarily as human. Instead of connecting ourselves to our common human roots, we have let our religious denominationalism become all-embracing. People are identified as Catholic or Protestant as a cultural identity rather than as members of a faith. We spontaneously think of ourselves in terms of what separates us, like animals that identify themselves with their den. The audiovisual world is one that mixes diverse peoples, yet our culture and churches do not. As humankind becomes conscious of itself as one body, it tears itself up in a struggle for identity. Instead of finding itself enriched by diversity, the human being is diluted and lost.

The explosion at the Russian atomic energy plant at Chernobyl sounded the alarm. For the first time in history, we can destroy our planet. There is no doubt that the mobilization of large ecological forces is necessary. From an evangelical perspective, however, the greatest danger is the loss, or the failure to emerge, of the spiritual life. Why should the world exist if it does not have a soul? For Jesus the life of the soul is more important than the physical life. "Do not fear those who kill the body but cannot kill the soul; rather fear him who can destroy both soul and body in hell" (Matthew 10:28). It is well known that in biblical thinking, different from Plato's thinking, the word *soul* means more than the breath of life; it characterizes that breath as dependent on God, intimately linked to the Spirit of God. According to Jesus, the worst evil for a human being is losing the inner principle that animates him from within, that belongs to his own breath and at the same time is linked to the Father. The loss of one's self is the greatest danger of the "new culture."

Exclusion from the World Marketplace

On the one hand we have the great skyscrapers of our cities, ultrasophisticated weapons, robots programmed to make cheaper and cheaper cars that go faster and faster. "Within thirty years the price of a computer has been divided by 8,000; if automobiles had experienced comparable progress, a car would today cost two dollars and would go as fast as sound."[8] On the one hand, there are countries that are underdeveloped, there are the unemployed, the flood of immigrants searching for work or driven from their countries, the young in the suburbs, senior citizens in rest homes, all of them seemingly with a mark on their forehead: "Useless!" They have lost not only their place in the world but their identity as well. On the great river of development robots reign, programmed by the superbrains and their great army of managers.

In today's world being human means very little; if one has no money, one is not recognized as a person. Without money one cannot cooperate in pushing the great mechanical world ahead. This is the second great misfortune of our time, brought about by the high degree of electronic technologies of production and globalization. People without money are marginalized and receive no recognition. They are excluded from the river of life.

The victims of the "new culture" are numerous. In his book *The*

End of Work, the American sociologist Jeremy Rifkin identifies unemployment as the great problem at the end of this century. Rifkin points out that in the United States in the 1960s, 33 percent of the population was workers. In 1995 workers made up only 17 percent of the population "although we produce more than any other country in the world."[9] By 2025, the number of workers should be only 2 percent of the population. Speaking later in the United States, Rifkin stated that as a consequence of this situation the only solution is a change in civilization. The new civilization must be centered on knowledge, family, and spiritual life.[10] Even though politicians tell us that there is light at the end of the tunnel, unemployment is inevitable in the near future. Any government plan to increase employment is only a coverup. When the *International Courier* reported on labor day on May 1, 1997, their story was titled "May 1st: The Defeat of Work."

Will Rifkin's prophecies come true? The twenty-first century will tell. Other disturbances may occur. There can be unexpected epidemics, an atomic disaster, a "rebellion of the slaves." Who can predict any other forms that may evolve? What ever they may be, two realities produced by the electronic era should be noticed.

First is the great disparity in the living conditions of the rich and the poor. We can speak of communication over the Internet, but what kind of communication is taking place and for whom? Eighty-five percent of Muslims are poor and 60 percent are uneducated or illiterate.[11] In 1997 98 percent of the users of the Internet were English speaking.[12] It is not as if the whole world will use the Internet tomorrow! We are facing a world in which those who die of hunger will not be the only problem. We are also facing a world in which the globalization of communications and economics will exclude those who are deprived of the means of participation, who do not move fast enough, who are not performing. In brief, they will be left out.

The people of Israel exiled in Babylon remembered Jerusalem and cried out to God because it was their fate to be taken to the banks of the Tigris and Euphrates Rivers. So today entire segments of the world population lament in exile. One must experience the stress of unemployment to speak of exclusion, when children begin to doubt their father, when their social circumstances change, moving into poorer housing and a more rundown neighborhood. How can we understand the young in the inner cities when they express themselves in films such as *Hatred* if we have not experienced being despised and broken in our will to be? Gangs are formed not for gratuitous violence, but for survival.

There are many forms of exclusion. In a society based on communication it takes a particular form. It does not simply mean that you do not receive a piece of the pie, but on a deeper level it means being left out of the groups who are creating a new world, to be sitting on the shore while the stream flows by. There are two major ways to acquire meaning in life. The first one, which has existed for centuries, consisted in being part of a group, to have a recognized place in the human community. This was the situation of people living in the villages of the past. Even the beggars and the sick were recognized and saw themselves as part of the community. The other way of having meaning today is electronic. It consists not only in being part of a group moving with the wind, participating in the improvement of society, but also in showing up and being able to move forward in the hit parade. When the whole world enters our living rooms through a hundred TV channels, our life begins to take on the dimensions of the television. To have a sense of solidarity with those who are close to us is no longer sufficient. What matters today is to be recognized in the marketplace of the world, to watch one's own image on screen, at least through the television remote control. In class, in the office, people hear of the Internet, of CD-ROMs, of virtual reality. When they see all the wonderful developments going on in the world, they cannot be content with a static sense of life tied to traditional values. People want to participate in the progress and in the collective applause of the world. Too many young people are uneasy because they do not believe they have a future. What gives sense to life today is being conscious of belonging to a group that is involved with the great currents of this time and with building the future.

What is at stake here is much more serious than the phenomenon of social and economic inequality. What we are facing is the death of the soul. Our soul is in danger of losing its life because no one is listening to it. It is a well known fact that in Asian countries losing face is tragic. There are some people who think it would be better to take one's own life than to lose face. This is a view that deserves our attention as it highlights how serious the sense of exclusion is. To be deprived of a place in the world means losing face—or losing one's image—and that means losing the very meaning of life. It is a feeling that is all the more intense in this time of TV and advertisements. Sociologists have taught us that for most of the human population the meaning of life is not granted by some intellectual principle or religious philosophy, but by sharing the destiny and objectives of a group. What is the meaning of my life if I am good for nothing, if I cannot work with those creating the future?

On the level of the material world death can be diagnosed by an electroencephalogram electronically tracing a flat line across a screen indicating that the brain has stopped functioning. On a more personal level, death can be experienced as the sense of abandonment when no one pays attention to you or expects nothing from you. It is a radical solitude. If no one pays any attention to me, I am dead. This is the first tragedy for outsiders. They experience death. The second tragedy is comparable to hell; they come to doubt in themselves, to be ashamed, to despise themselves. Simone Weil says the worst thing that Christ suffered on the cross was not the physical pain, but his sense of being abandoned. When people see themselves as abandoned by others, they feel as if God himself abandons them. Of course, most outsiders do not think so deeply. For the most part people have the experience of belonging to a group, as marginal as it may be. But the warning remains. Those who want to bring the Gospel to the marginalized must see the poison that infects people who are outsiders, the slope they are rolling down and its extent.

—) Good News?

Graffiti on walls, billboards and bumper stickers on the roads that say "Jesus Saves!" "God loves you!" Is this the Good News? Of course the phrase is true, but this is hardly the way to express it. To the bad news about the outsiders we have discussed above neither our actions, empty slogans, nor preaching can be the answer. Only the facts will speak and have the right impact. The generation that has grown up on TV images and sounds is like those in the Gospels who demand miracles, only ready to believe in what they see. How can we evangelize them? What should we say or do?

In the following pages I will develop ideas on how we should understand the "new culture" and the "message of the Good News."

I will try to show how we might travel the paths of a new dialogue of evangelization and culture.

The following four steps outline the fundamental process.

1. You can express the Good News only if you feel deeply and emotionally the major stresses of today. Feeling and sharing them come first.

2. Perform "miracles."

3. Offer an experience of salvation through personal relationships and an environment able to transform the interior life of the person.

4. After the experience, explain. Faith must be given a foundation.

Feeling the Stresses of the Time

Some people are obsessed with giving answers. They think that every problem has a solution and they know what that solution is. They sometimes even proclaim it with authority. These preachers can convince the weak and, of course, manipulate them. Unfortunately their strategies work. It is sad that the tactics of evangelization must take a deviation that is so remote from the glory of God and man.

Evangelization according to Christ means primarily that the evangelizer has personally felt the great movements, the basic questions, the rebellions, and the aspirations of the time. Understanding the era and understanding one's self should go hand in hand. We must somehow experience the temptation of the world and the pain caused by failure. Since people today are accustomed to the emotional language of radio and TV it is all the more important that evangelizers have an affective commitment to communicating the Gospel. People are not looking for intellectual solutions to their problems. Rather people are looking for evangelizers who communicate in ways that show they are giving themselves to the other. I believe that we cannot reveal the Gospel without revealing ourselves, sharing through our fears, exhausting ourselves for the sake of the other.

We cannot speak effectively to others simply by giving answers to questions. They cannot help but see our sincerity in our eyes and hear it in our tone of voice. The speech that we use should be no less than what we use when in communion with God.

Performing "Miracles"

The language of the media returns us to the Gospel in its beginning. In his book *The Church Jesus Wanted,* the biblical exegete Gerard Lohfink asks us to change the way we understand miracles. It is a mistake to think that Jesus would first give a speech, and then perform a miracle to prove the truthfulness of his words. No, says Lohfink, we have miracles first. The Kingdom of God is the miracle as are the healings and the retreat of evil.[13] Commenting on the Gospels Eugen Drewermann stresses the same idea in his own way. "I would like it to do exactly . . . what Jesus himself entrusted to his disciples to do. . . . He told them only to lay hands on the people, to heal the sick and to expel evil spirits. Today we would say it means to liberate the people from their neuroses and psychoses. Only when this is done are the evangelizers able to tell the people how close to God they are. There are always people who come to us feeling lost and burdened with psychological distress. If we as priests, ministers or theologians can only say 'Jesus loves you,' or 'Jesus was the son of God,' we are sending them back to the place from where Jesus wanted to draw them."[14]

How should we understand the meaning of a miracle? I suggest that in the context of audiovisual language, the notion of miracle should be broadened. Miracles should be understood as a spiritual emanation of a person. We should not forget the biblical meaning of miracle, an unexpected sign that especially shows the presence of God and his saving action.[15] Not everyone is called to perform miracles. Yet cannot even the smallest children perform little miracles, miracles in the broadest sense? By that I mean the gestures, the bodily movements, the look of a child that can drive evil out of others. Isn't it in some way a miracle when a sick person receives a gesture of tenderness, some sign of caring from a nurse that helps him or her sleep better than any pill would?

In the audiovisual world we learn the impact of the eyes, of gestures, of modulations of the voice. We learn how this impact can be strengthened by the use of a microphone and by skillful lighting. The fundamental language of the Gospel is not words alone but "the power that had gone forth from him (Mark 5:30). The expression of power in looks or gestures shows what we have experienced through our undertakings and the scars from our fights. Strange and quite characteristic in this era of the media is the study of the Kirlian effect, a sort of aura or emanation from people that shows up on a photographic plate. A specialist in Taiwan has created a system of electronic amplification enabling him to shoot in color the personal aura radiating from people. This suggests that people have some form of impact on their surroundings. Whatever the exact nature of these phenomena may be, notice the language. Our body speaks, creates anxiety or peace, hope or depression; in this sense we can expel evil spirits and bring the sick back into the community.

So what is the secret of these little miracles? Faith; it is the amount of faith going into our simplest gestures, giving them a supernatural impact. This is the faith that impels one to undertake new ordering actions. Performing miracles means connecting one's self with the almighty power of God, giving him our body to wake people up. This is the language of the Gospel and it touches hearts most intimately.

Offering an Experience of Salvation

Those who feel left out or lost are like the sick appearing in the Gospel of John expecting the swirling of water in the pool of Bethesda (see John 5:2–9). They expect the swirling of a twofold experience, that of a new alliance with God that reintroduces them to the community, and that of the Christian community bringing them to the rebirth in faith.

In an old eastern African tradition, healing means introducing the sick person back into the community, back into the circle of life, into the marketplace. Such healing is accomplished through an experience of new relationships and reconciliation. The Gospel is an experience of a "new alliance" with God, with one's self, and with others. What form does this alliance take? It is the worker priests, those religious men and women who went out to share the lives of the poorest of the poor. It is the simple and unknown gestures of one who truly listens to others. It is the one who struggles to find jobs for the unemployed. Charitable organizations tell us something of the alliance of God with his people. The issue here is not to act like a sociologist; it is to be proactive in the way that Confucius places above all others, to practice the virtue of humanness through which we make our own the viewpoint that of the other.[16] Christians will speak of charity; the way of charity will be defined by Jesus Christ.

At the top of the experience of alliance lies the Christian community. To be concrete we will recall and interpret the Taizé experience. Taizé with its old Romanesque church is on a hill in Burgundy, with thousands of young people climbing up in buses or walking, with loaded knapsacks. Taizé is neither unique nor flawless, but it does provide a place of silence where I am surrounded in sound. Taizé has archetypal value. In its fifty years of outreach the experience of Taizé has proven itself, placing its experience between outbursts of affection and intellectual dryness. On every continent it has created a network, communicating and praying even through the Internet. I even recommend the Taizé experience to those who attend our Center for the Research and Training in Social and Religious Communication (CREC-AVEX). There you will see that participating in an audiovisual world is not a means, but a way of being. There you will see the future of religion. You will uncover faith in this time of media and of the "young without borders."

The Taizé experience allows the right side of the brain to become predominant. A receptive attitude is more important than activity. Music is predominant over speech, silence over the word, welcoming others over judging them. Experiencing our common humanity is more important than being Indian, German, or American. Songs and polyphonic instruments echo unity in a well of diversity. The buildings are simple and even crude; meals are built around rice and biscuits. On Friday night Roger Schutz, the founder and prior, spreads butter on slices of bread and gives them out to the young people crowded around him. In this simple gesture he expresses the essence of the message, the Last Supper, the new family—not only disciples but also friends.

Praying during the night in the church with all of these young people, some of them lying prostrate on the ground, I cannot help but think of what Nicodemus said to Jesus: "How can anyone be born after having grown old? Can one enter a second time into the mother's womb and be born?" (John 3:4). Taizé is like a big mother's womb where it is possible for a young person in search of identity to listen to the inner voices and consequently to be born again. This is the secret of Taizé, the unconditional welcome, the expression of arm sympathy, the freedom of being one in diversity. Taizé is the ground of a rebirth of one's self, according to the spirit of Christ. ("Ground" in its full sense, which we discuss in the next chapter.) In that chiaroscuro church, filled with warm speech and surrounding music, lit by the glow of many candles, these biblical sentences are sung repeatedly, "Who am I, what do I want?" Participants feel the closeness of the community of Taizé, inviting everyone to wondering peace.

Here God is not the answer, but is the source of the question. Adults impatiently say to me, "The services are too long! Always the same unending songs!" Experiencing the same service a young person will say, "I remained in the church until 3:00 a.m." Is it possible to get bored at the beach, resting there and swimming?

Taizé is, of course, Brother Roger, the archetypes of the father and the wise man, but also the prophet surrounded by little children foretelling the future of humankind. Taizé is the ecumenical community of the brothers revealing the existence of happier and more fundamental links than those of blood, money, or social consideration. Not a community of group dynamics or psychology, it is a community on the call of the Father on high that mutually acknowledges our various vocations.

Did I make the "Taizé experience" too attractive? No! I speak from long personal experience and because Taizé is known all over the world. Taizé provides young people an experience of the Gospel that efficiently meets the needs of young people who are addressing the vacuity of life, the lack of a future, the lack of meaning in life, and the feeling of being an outcast. The Taizé experience is not words, but the experience of belonging to a "body." Not speeches about the love of God but an experience of reconciliation and of Christian community. Not intercultural considerations, but a concrete organization with an international network.

After the Experience, Explain

It is not possible to envisage a purely audiovisual communication of the faith. To do so would show disrespect for the human person, undervalue people by limiting them to right-brain stimulation. It is true that the impact of print in human development should soften, but it should not disappear. Through his journeys and encyclicals, Pope John Paul II gives a good example of balancing the two, even if the journeys are more effective than the encyclicals for evangelization.

When should we speak? When should we catechize? This is a

complex question depending on the character of the speaker and the listeners. They have to be sensitive to teachable situations and the grace of the moment. I would only suggest that in this era of the media, when the right half of the brain is predominant, the gesture, the miracle, precede teaching. People must have the sense that God loves them before he can be proclaimed and explained. This is valid for children as well. One reason that religious instruction has so little effect on their lives is that the words they hear do not penetrate good soil. As a moral and social superstructure, catechesis is presented that does not meld with their inner experiences. The answer is not to abolish the catechism but to root it in experience.

I hesitate to comment on what should be taught in a classroom. My main concern is that the words we teach are not reaching the heart of the students. Before we can communicate the Church's teaching, we must translate it into words that make sense in the context of a lived spiritual experience.

1. "I am." The "I" is in me a unique and sacred mystery, which no one else can touch. The Source of the "I" is God, "Our Father." This fundamental illumination keeps me grounded and confident in the turmoils of life.

2. The "I" is recognized and loved as it is, sick or marginal. The "I" is given space. The "I" recognizes the forgiveness of God even if I am a criminal. The church, the Christian community, is a place where I am accepted as I am.

3. The "I" has a future even beyond death. The "I" is called to be happy and to "bear fruit." Through Christ, the "I" finds the meaning behind suffering, death and hope.

4. The world is on the way toward unity and reconciliation. This is God's plan revealed in the Bible and by Christ. We can have a sense of elation recognizing that under the influence of the Holy Spirit, we can be part of this movement.

5. We can be comforted by the experience of the Church, the living presence of our master Christ, and the help of the Holy Spirit. The community of brothers and Christian celebrations already model the fullness of life possible on earth.

—) **The Success of the Gospel?**

Success will be costly for the men and women who dare to proclaim the Gospel in this new world. To tell the truth, I think that they are scared stiff at the prospect. It is always more comfortable to fall back on doctrinal orthodoxy, to preserve the "deposit of faith" than to proclaim the Gospel so that it impacts the world. The temptation is to make comfortable noises that do not risk anything instead of being dangerously successful in shaking people up in the marketplace. Jesus was correct when he said, "the children of this age are more shrewd . . . than are the children of light" (Luke 16:8). The "New Age" shaking the Church may be an opportunity for a renewal of its mission.

If we are tuned to God's voice in our innermost being as well as the world around us, the Gospel and success can go together.

Evangelizing in the era of the media means producing the effect of Christ amplified by electronics.

—) **Questions for Reflection**

1. What can we learn from St. Paul about proclaiming the Gospel in our culture?

2. Is it possible to speak about the Gospel in terms of success?

3. Is an understanding of the cross paramount in your life? What explicit impact does it have for you and your ministry?

4. What impact has the electronic culture had on your attempts at nurturing faith and/or faith communities?

5. "With the life we live, we lose our inner being." How so? What can we do about it?

6. Are there new ways to effectively minister to youth who are affected by the media culture?

7. Does the electronic culture have anything to offer our "becoming as persons"?

8. What new insights concerning evangelization have been stimulated by reflecting on this chapter?

The Shaken-Up Church

> When the figure is predominant, as in the written medium, one goes
> directly to the ideas, to the intellectual content. The sensory and
> affective impact is peripheral and most of the time unconscious.
> When the ground—the background, the audiovisual medium,
> is predominant, the message is grasped not primarily by
> the intellect, but by the effect produced on the
> senses and the whole psyche.

Every time I enter St. Peter's Basilica in Rome, I walk around that big nave marveling at its harmonious and gigantic dimensions. My eyes invariably go up below the vault to a striking text in a glorious context. It says, "Simon, Simon, Satan had gotten his wish to sift you like wheat, but I have prayed for you, Simon, that your faith may not fail, and once you have recovered, you in your turn must strengthen your brothers" (Luke 22:31–32). Also tied to the triumph of the Church is a warning: "For you who think you are strong, the cock is going to crow!"

This seems to me to be a text that perfectly fits the situation of the Church today. Through the ages, the Church of Christ has been sifted like wheat. While the "new culture" springing out of the world of electronics is being born, the Church is, and will be, terribly shaken up. The image used by Jesus is that of separating wheat from the chaff on a windy day in order to separate the grain from the straw, dust, and scraps. A change in culture is the permission given to Satan, not to destroy the Church, but to shake it up in order to purify its faith and open its horizons.

There is no need to imagine Satan as some small devil with horns.

Let us rather think in terms of the impact of the weather and the wind. The infinite connections of electronics are producing powerful energies, especially from the falling of borders and the violent vibrations of images and sounds. Is not Satan somehow similar to electronics? Is he not Lucifer, the prince of lights, with bright, attractive commercials? Is not Satan the great producer of special effects? It was never possible to prove the continual influence of subliminal messages hidden in some hard-rock music and recordings. What is certain is that the little electronic god gives a kind of shock to humankind: election, violence, and seduction. Such is the releasing of winds for better or for worse, which can be named Satan here.

I have no intention of playing the role of some kind of Nostradamus. I am merely suggesting here (I would not dare say revealing), that the new situation carries with it a mixture of glory and weakness for the Church and for the Gospel. My reflection here is inspired by the theses of Harold Innis and Marshall McLuhan. The most determining factor to give a structure to societies, to change cultures and civilizations, lies in a major technological invention in the field of communication.[1] The Roman documents *Redemptoris Missio* and *Aetatis Novae* have resumed the same vision. The media are more than means; they are a "New Age" of the world, and they determine a "new culture." (Note: Here the word *culture* is meant in the general anthropological sense: the whole of the ways in which the human community solves the problems of making sense of the world and the place of humanity within it.) Never in history has the world of language and communication been so shaken up as in today's electronic world. Consequently it is normal that the Church should be shaken up as well. Now we have to face this world and make our contribution for the widening and deepening of the presence of the Church.

It will not be easy to explain the influence of the electronic culture on our church in a few pages. That interaction is just starting. It is indeed possible to identify the new technologies and to see their material consequences; for instance, the invasion of the Internet throughout the world. I will rather try to indicate here some major cultural consequences—the changes of attitude, which I think are the most serious. These are ones that I think are most effectively shaking up the tradition of the Church. New communications technologies and the media are primarily cultural agitators. New opinions, ways of thinking, ways of living, for example, keeping the radio or television on all day long, challenge the accepted ideas and current practices of our churches. There is an irresistible and practical underground philosophy now challenging traditional wisdom. I sum it up somewhat humorously in three short maxims that will bring to mind some ways of being and thinking that are silently influencing consciousness and daily behavior.

I have obviously chosen these maxims because they issue directly from the practice of the media. But they are also distanced from the practices of the Church for several centuries. I have gleaned them when working with television producers. The first comes from Father Demierre, a priest in charge of religious programs on French-language Swiss television. I have also been strongly influenced by lengthy discussion with Marshall McLuhan. While he used complex explanations, the "prophet of the media" had a genius for these terse and suggestive phrases.

⎯⎯) **1.** The "Ground" Is More Important Than the Figure

"Ground" is a word used also in French, in German *Grund*. Novelist Milan Kundera stressed the importance of this term and how difficult it is to translate because it "has nothing to do with a Latin way of thinking."[2] I have analyzed the notion of "ground" more technically in *Language and Culture of the Media*.[3] This term expresses an approach to things, a global intuition rather than a precisely objective reality. It is at the same time land and process, foundation and environment, context and raison d'etre. In a photograph, the "ground" is the composition of lines, the balance of volumes, the location of the most important person, the rhythm of light and contrast that should determine the value of the message. Let us say that in the language of the media, the land, the environment, is more important than the focal point to which the eyes are directed. Or in more psychological terms, what stays in the background of consciousness determines more than does that which moves in the foreground.

From my perspective, this statement is doubtless the most upsetting. It is the most revolutionary for a person from a Western academic and literary culture. It is also disquieting for the Church. We were taught in school that the message lies in the word. It can be found in the logical connection between words and punctuation within a sentence. "Understand the words, understand the sentence and the links between the sentences. Then you will grasp the message."

The media people arrive and turn the system upside down. Albert Mehrabian, an expert on television, writes, "On television what a person says represents only 7 percent of what is communicated. Thirty-eight percent is conveyed by the way of expressing one's self (voice, vocabulary, rhythm of speech) and 55 percent by the expressions in the face and the movement of the body."[4]

If such a statement is proven true, is it in opposition directly to the practice of the Church? After the Council of Trent, the Church founded its communication on learning clear formulas and in well-defined doctrine. Think of the *Catechism of the Council of Trent,* canon law (the term is significant), and seminaries demanding a strict intellectual formation! It is because the fundamental conditions of today's evangelization are at stake. The seriousness of ecclesial turmoil of the new makes it more important to understand "ground" and figure. In my opinion, if we include with the ideal of "ground" that of modulation (as we will do later on), we can say that the theory of the primacy of the "ground" in the language of the media constitutes the main disturbance for the Church.

To the people who are trained in communication, we say that modulation and "ground" are two columns of audiovisual electronic communication. You will not understand anything if you do not grasp that structure of communication. You can of course act without understanding, but in order to understand the laws of this new language, you have to integrate these categories. Without understanding these categories you cannot understand yourself and your time, the infatuation with Eastern thought, feminism, or modern painting. Since the sixties, a slow change has been taking place in the pastoral work of the Church. A new balance between text and context, between right- and left-brain influence, between academics and charismatics is being sought. It is necessary to grapple with its value and its opportunities while keeping in mind its risks and conditions. Can a theology of the primacy of the "ground" be accepted in communicating the Gospel? That is the question. I will propose some concrete examples of different approaches.

The First Approach:
Marie Claire, or The format is more
important than the text

When I read a book, the message is found in the text. The words hit my consciousness. I ask myself questions like, "What did it mean? Did I understand it well: is it true? Is it compatible with all that I already know?" Here the words represent the "figure," that is the form or situation in the forefront of my thought, the focus of my consciousness. In a writing culture the words come first, like consciousness and ideas.

Now we have the media people. Jean Provoust founded the magazine *Marie Claire* in 1937. This audiovisual genius upset the formula for the way magazines were published. "Primarily, I wanted beautiful paper, glossy paper. I wanted a magazine that would create a style of readers by its texture, its pictures, and its brightness. The women buying *Marie Claire* will unconsciously buy a beautiful dress. They will buy it to acquire class. I wanted to make all French women middle-class people."

Jean Provoust has succeeded! His magazine is still in print with several international editions. It does not mean that the text is unimportant. But the paper, the style, the atmosphere, the graphics and the pictures, the rhythm of black and white, the displays, the focus on celebrities, the system of distribution are what matters above all. This not only sells the magazine, but also has the strongest effect on the reader. I call that the "ground," a ground that is the glossy paper and commands the form.

Here appears the shifting sense of the term "message." For people of the written word, the message means intellectual content. It lies in the words. It is both logical and unconscious. The alphabetic medium with its linear and abstract character favors the intellectually clear consciousness. For media people the message is found in the effect on behavior. This is both logical and unconscious. By maximizing its sensory character, the audiovisual medium favors perception through the senses and their effect on the body. Now what shakes up the body's behavior is more in the appearance of the page than in the words. It is the hum of the images, the frequency modulation and its easy listening.

When the figure is predominant, as in the written medium, one goes directly to the ideas, to the intellectual content. The sensory and affective impact is peripheral and most of the time unconscious. When the ground, the background, the audiovisual medium, is predominant, the message is grasped not primarily by the intellect, but by the effect produced on the senses and the whole psyche. Of course, when I watch a movie, I listen to the words and I perceive images that I decipher in my consciousness. But that conscious perception is caused 80 percent by sounds, vibrations, rhythms shaking up my senses and affectivity without necessarily having a link to the meaning of the words and the images. Such is precisely the function of symbolic audiovisual language. When I see a Coca-Cola ad, there is no intellectual link between Coca-Cola and a youth diving into the water. The link is in the effects that are produced. Coca-Cola should have the same effects as a young person diving into water. "The word and image are symbolic," writes C. G. Jung, "when they imply something more than their obvious and immediate meaning."[5]

In the language of the ground, I understand first of all the effect produced on the senses. In the language of the figure, I understand through the intellectual interpretation of signs abstracted twice. The symbols of sounds are the letters of the alphabet.

The Second Approach: The Walkman, or Modulation is more important than words

I have explained the meaning of the term Modulation and the reasons for choosing it in *The New Era in Religious Communication*.[6] In brief, modulation means vibrations varying in frequency. It is a technical term deliberately chosen to characterize the essential nature of media language. Unlike writing with its twofold abstract signs (letters and sound), vibrations are the most sensory signs in existence. Sound and visual vibrations take their first meaning from the way they affect the body.

Wasn't the inventor of the Walkman crazy? How could he have imagined that people would walk in the streets with headsets stuck in their ears? But the president of Sony had the idea. When he proposed manufacturing the device, his engineers did not take him seriously. Probably without consciously knowing it, he understood the weight of the "ground." He knew that for the young generation of media users, the more you could shake the senses up, the more there was a message and pleasure. Understanding electronic audiovisual language, he was not seeking to impact the intellect, but to create an effect on the senses. He wanted music to become a body-to-body experience, a listening in private, and a shaking up of the nervous system. This effect should produce those powerful rock-and-roll atmospheres in which the gathered group stands up and becomes one dancing body. Such is the language of the "ground," of sensitive bodies shaking and touching each other. With a Walkman, listening to music touches me so physically that I somehow become the music and my muscles move in spite of myself.

It is a language from the bottom, made of an organization of sounds, images, texture, rhythms, places, so that the body is moved to the utmost. It is the language of the people, the language of politics, the language from Eastern countries, the language of banquets and feasts. This is the predominant language of the first evangelization, the language calling us to become a disciple. How could we not rejoice in the progress of the audiovisual as a major opportunity for evangelization?

When we are told that St. John Vianney, the curé of Ars, was spending his nights preparing his sermons, we can imagine that he was working on his ideas and words. This is probably true. But what is more important is that while keeping awake, unconsciously, he controlled his breathing, he sharpened his soul, and he sculpted his face. Father Lacordaire, the famous preacher, was asked, "What did you see at Ars?" He answered, "I saw someone saying the 'Our Father.'"

The Third Approach:
The Thief, or The background
is easy to manipulate

Have you experienced being violently jostled when you are leaving a bus or a subway train? Once you are out, you look for your purse, but it has vanished. The thief distracted you by jostling you, and while you thought about your painful arm, he took your wallet from your pocket. A thief will never steal the "figure." A tourist to whom we had lent a camera to visit Rome assured us that he would come back with it. On a bus he was holding the camera tightly.

"Nobody will steal it from me!" Back in his hotel room he had the camera all right, but his wallet had been stolen. It was part of the "ground," the background of his consciousness. The game of the thief is similar. If the thing he intends to steal is presently in the forefront of your consciousness, he manages to shift it to the background. He is going to jostle you on the bus so that you are suddenly attentive to the impact and are not paying attention to your purse.

This last example shows another aspect of media-oriented communication, namely, its impact on the unconscious. This language shocks us. It is the most powerful language to strengthen or modify behavior, to put rationality to sleep and lead ideas and belief to other angles. The language is both wonderful and dangerous. Wonderful if it serves what the Bible calls the "heart" and also calls "more than reason." It is dangerous if it destroys wisdom and the healthy intelligence of reality. The sensory, emotional impact of the media is so strong, so physical that it can hide reality entirely or at least change in depth its perception and intelligence. When you watch the big celebrations put on by the dictator of North Korea to celebrate his birthday, you can understand that the sensory impact is so strong and violent that the population loses its sense of reality. Still more serious is that the personal consciousness is alienated. The ground can alter the states of consciousness in depth, in the same way a hypnotic drug does. I think that one of the major objectives of the media training in school is to make the mediatic "ground" more clearly understood, so that its styles, formats, laws of language, unconscious symbol, the unknown economic process, come into the front of the mind.

The Background,
the First Language of Evangelization

We will not elaborate here a philosophical theory aiming at demonstrating the primacy of the "ground" over the "figure." Let us situate ourselves in the concrete. Can the wonderful Gospel entrusted to Christians by the Lord be communicated by the content, the ground, and the background even better than by words? I think that for the media generation the place from which one speaks, the tone of voice, the conviction, and the emotion springing up from the heart are more important than words. The global scenery within which we can situate ourselves, the festive atmosphere, the joy of singing, the sick and the handicapped people who are here, the walls, the chairs or the trees, the type of music and lighting are the first conditions for evangelization. These are not only the first conditions, but they are the first and best language. This is the ground: the background of relationships, the stress on words that shows conviction, the cleanness and beauty of the place. All of these so-called surroundings of the message are the message itself. The message in the fundamental and mediatic sense is that of the signal, modulation itself causing an effect. Indeed, the ground is not the whole of the message. It is the most important element of it, though the words are more apt to make thought more precise. Of what use would be a message that is not communicated, a salt that does not salt?

The example of Pope John Paul II is a good example of the value of this language. When the pope visited France for the first time, a young woman, a business secretary, baptized but inactive, expressed to me her burning desire to see him. This meant a journey of over 1000 kilometers and a night sleeping out in the open. Upon her return she told me how enthusiastic she was. "At last, someone who keeps on the road! Don't you see that this world is going mad if it stays on this course?" Seeing her excitement, I invited her to speak in front of theology students at Lyon's Catholic University. After having heard her, the students skeptically asked, "And when the pope speaks of the pill, of pleasure, do you still agree?" Her answer was categorical. "Yes! Absolutely!" Knowing that she was a person who behaved according to her own sense of freedom, I asked her for some explanations. She spoke to me of the necessity of having in our time a man who stands up to the abuses and general neglect of society. To my concrete question about the pill, she answered with a kind of indignation. "But finally, I have a conscience. I know what I must do!"

Here we find the message of the "ground." Some theologians told me later, "It is too easy, they listen to the song, but not to the words. It is ineffective." Yes, she did follow the song and the rhythms more than the words. To speak of her experience in audiovisual language, even the words were image and music for her. Her way of speaking of the pope is symptomatic. She recalled his gestures, the force of his expressions, and his way of holding the cross. The young theologians were right. The woman was following the song. Their mistake was in thinking that it was ineffective. Following an image and a song, following the "ground," can often be tremendously effective. The woman has a much-improved Christian life and has asked me to give to her a serious preparation for marriage.

Do you want to try to put the Gospel in the marketplace? Spend more time with the background than with the face. In the past teachers taught from the illustration or the explanation. Today we go from the image of the music to the word. After twenty years of radio, of the Walkman and television, people do not hear in the same way. They do not approach reality from the same point of view. The word remains the word, a fortress of thought, but it does not occupy the same mental space. These changes do not put the mission of the Church fundamentally at stake. In the long run it will be more beneficial for the Church to be drawn back to the ways of communication in which the Gospel was first preached. Nevertheless how can the churches, both Catholic and Protestant, not experience some hard times because they are so tied to Gutenberg's culture? The Gospel has been translated into national languages. Time has now come to translate into a "ground" language and so recover a balance in communication between the Church and the world.

Danger! The objections to this new environment are well known. It is a manipulative environment, superficial, lacking in structure, reducing Christianity to pleasure, deviations toward sects, and other failings. How can we embark on this journey taking chances while avoiding its dangers? The discernment is done by intellectual clarification (reasoning), but even more by a daily regimen of meditation on the Gospel and opening up to the international community.

Through sound and visual effects, young people can be interested and even aroused to fanaticism and become a sect. Through flags, labels, and localized religious songs, there can become a nationalistic Catholicism. Is that the Spirit of Christ? The first condition is that of audiovisual display; the organization of worship places would be the product not only of good technicians and architects, but also of professionals who are spiritual as well as being spiritually in agreement with the Church. The building of a space for both sound and sight would be the fruit of the Spirit of Christ living in community, gathering prophets, professionals, artist and audience, a community that, albeit localized, is thinking in a "universal" way and preparing for the "global village."

Someone may ask, "Can we use a rock band to liven up the Sunday liturgy so that young people can be attracted?"

Attract the students to what? For what? Will the rock band with its display of lights and sound draw young people to an encounter with Christ and with what is dwelling in their innermost being? Will the great celebration with band and T-shirts somehow arouse the taste of Christ? Will it help give birth to the small interior voice of liberation and love? We agree that we should go in stages, with communicators asking themselves three fundamental questions.

- Does the proposed atmosphere come from the Spirit of Christ or the spirit of domination?

- Does it fit a progressive awakening of the inner life of the people or will it simply lead to external behaviors?

- Is it faithful to the images, the style, and the words of the Bible? Is it linked to the traditions of the Church?

Will it create a sect? The test for distinguishing the climate and the process of evangelization from that of a sect is the following one. Do the participants listen to other opinions? Do they share other spiritual environments? Are they open to other teachers? Of course even more than religious education, evangelization requires moments of affective intensity. There are experiences of becoming conscious of what happens in the fire, but reasoning as well as being open must follow, introducing other opinions and other spiritual environments.

The Communicator Must Become Grounded It is important that communicators should be able to speak the language of the "ground." They must especially increase their capabilities through the wonderful resources of the audiovisual world. The use of electronics increases our possibilities of "content" as has never happened in history. The right creative and spiritual "ground" is difficult to find. It cannot be insignificant, neither too strong nor too weak. This is an imperative training that is not given in Catholic seminaries. The Orthodox churches are better oriented on this point. For them the formation of the voice and the formation of icons are essential. Along with their intellectual studies, their voices are changed little by little to express an inner religious resonance. Liviu, a member of the Faculty of Theology in Bucharest, told me that while voices are amplified through electronics, these remain a "poor relation" to the development of the human voice expressing a deep inner religious reso-

nance. If the reader accepts what we have said here, we have to create spiritual formation of the ground, with schools integrating Spirit,
body, and proper technique in training the voice.

—) 2. In the Media, the Signal Belongs to the Transmitter; the Message Belongs to the Receiver

Clearly, in the media the audience decides the timeliness, the importance, and the meaning of the message.

The receivers are the masters of the message in two ways. First,
by switching the message on, by interpreting the message from where
they are and from the milieu that molded them. So the popular songs
tell us the truth is asleep inside us. The laws of the market economy
are recognized in this maxim. We will speak of them later. Without
knowing it, the public applies these laws to religion and culture. What
can be bought is good; what is successful is true. Aside from the
improper shifting of the market laws to define what is good and true,
that maxim is based in the very nature of the media, using sound and
image. Words and figures are the least ambiguous. Conversely, image,
voice, environment—because they aim at the senses—are highly
questionable. By their very nature images, especially if they are symbolic, are open to a thousand interpretations. Most probably this is
what Pius XII meant when he said, "The faith is in great danger of
being lost in a civilization of image."

How can the Church accommodate an expression giving priority
to subjective interpretation?

Of course there is no way to complacently ratify the cultural data
of the media era. The truth is not engendered by the "ratings box" or
by the power, or by affective pressures, or by individual subjectivity.
It is born from the Holy Spirit, the Spirit who (for Catholics), is
received in the community of believers. The warrant of the truth is
not the law of the biggest numbers, but the communion with the universal Church.

That short maxim enlightens us on three points:

• First, the maxim is right in the sense that it is not easy to judge
   the value of the significance of the mediatic message. With
   examinations we can judge how well the verbal teaching of a

professor is understood. But how can we explain the nonverbal message? If the image is more powerful than the words, it is probably because it can be interpreted in different ways by each individual listener. How could we not respect it? Resuming the reflection of a sociologist on the effects of television, I would say: the message depends on the person who listens, at what time, at what place, with whom he is listening, what he has eaten and when, what he is drinking while listening, what he is doing later, what groups he belongs to, what his nature is, whether he is sleepy. It is natural that such a message belongs to the receiver more than the transmitter.

- Second, the communicator must always keep in mind that the listener handles a fearsome weapon, the TV remote control. This weapon is not simply a trivial electronic tool. It is an extension of a freedom and self-consciousness that has grown considerably since the mid-twentieth century. The TV remote control means respect for the psychological condition and the situations of life, the ability to choose, and the granting of autonomy.

- Finally Christians today must learn how to be faithful to a pluralism of interpretations, to say "I" in communion. The values of individual and religious freedom are growing quickly in our time. The maxim helps us to understand and rejoice in this situation. But such a development will have to go hand in hand with the responsibility for seeking truth and communion. Here a new balance should be found between the affirmation of one's self and the concern for truth and communion.

─) 3. Too Many Figures, No Figure Any More

Marshall McLuhan used to apply this maxim to the electronic multiplication of messages. Messages are so numerous today that there is no message any more. "When by using a photocopy machine everyone can make a book, there is no book anymore." Day after day, when a lot of information hits the consciousness, there is no information and no recall. Everything becomes a vast landscape, or perhaps a thick soup from which some pieces emerge to be eaten one after the other.

What follows? Today the audience is more important than the speaker. By audience I mean both the number of listeners and its organization in networks. (Note: the word *network,* coming etymologically from fishing net, points to a flexible structure of people communicating with one anther around common interests.) The audience embodies the message, puts it in the forefront, dictates its importance, and alters its meaning. When conducting a seminar in New Delhi, India, I was invited to participate in the celebration of India's Independence Day. As early as 5 a.m. we arrived at a huge piece of land and sat down on the ground, behind long barriers. The crowd of about one million people gathered and waited for three or four hours, without anything to do but wait. At last Indira Gandhi, the prime minister of India, rode by standing in a convertible car, wearing a beige sari, arms raised to greet the crowd. We saw her for no more than fifteen seconds. What would Indira Gandhi be without the audience of a million people waiting in the dust for three hours? What would the pope be without the Vatican and the crowds acclaiming him? Who are we if no one is waiting for us? One of the modern laws of media communication is to think of diffusion before creation, audience before words, and network before writing. Not only to seek for the needs of the listeners, but also to give greater meaning to the words.

The Internet

The Internet demonstrates the primordial importance of the network, of its equality and its extension. Belonging is more important than intellectually adhering to a message, to adhere to that network as to a nation, first physically by accepting its laws and saluting its flag. So it is very important for Americans to vitalize the Internet. By so doing, using their language (90 percent is in English), by their programs and process of functioning, they integrate the confused clients to American ways. It is the network that gives body to the word.

It has always struck me that a sort of religion was growing up around the Internet. It has a process of initiation, and the people who respond with fervor gather as "communicants." Why? What causes so much interest in the Internet? It is important to understand not only the Internet, but also how the Church might situate itself on the Internet. From the start, in its conception as a military net in the

United States, it is a network of networks, a huge net making it possible, in case of a disaster, to address thousands of nerve endings to which all information can circulate. This perspective remains. For the new user the Internet is primarily an immense territory giving access to all the goods of knowledge and the virtual world of human relationships. It is a territory covered with so many figures that there is no figure any more except the one that you are looking for, directed by your interests.

In that sense the Internet will provide a lot of services at a relatively cheap price, to schools, research enterprises, administrations. The "Intranet," a formula being developed for use within firms, will facilitate the private and very quick exchanges within a group; the benefits are obvious for all organizations and consequently for the Church. How could we not use them? I do not think that these services are sufficient to explain the fever for the Internet, especially in the younger generation. There is an ideology—some will say a messianism—around the Internet.

I see three reasons for this: the pleasure of surfing the Net; the pleasure of having a world connection; and the pleasure of the utopia.

- First of all there is the pleasure of playing. The Internet is a great tracking game. Its ground is not the forest, but the computer screen, moving, glistening, with bright colors and sounds. It is fascinating. What I see on the screen is always a beautiful image of myself. Even if what I write is false and tasteless, the image is beautifully graphic and organized by me (or so I believe). By surfing or writing on the screen, I put on brand-new clothing at every moment. It is nothing like an austere sheet of paper! The habit of running here and there online, of choosing between thousands of possibilities, of reacting immediately, of hearing and seeing simultaneously creates—if only unconsciously—a psychology whose key words are pleasure, game, curiosity, luck, dialogue, pure stimulation of the moment, lack of duration. I can also recall its shadow side: narcissism, self-eroticism, and individualism. The fact is that the Internet generation has the taste for learning by playing, by curiosity, by interest, by modulation. Many Church leaders are staying away from the Internet because they think too much in terms of teaching the Catechism or preaching. They have not seen that the message could be a pleasure, stimulation, an interaction, and a sudden shock—like love at first sight—at the turning point of a race.

• Second, the Internet causes the whole world to take a breath. Getting a place on the World Wide Web means staking out part of the major adventure of the time. It is a widening of one's self, participating actively in communication, at last free and planetary. Sociologists have taught us that for most of the population, the sense of life is not given by ideas or doctrines, but by participating in a group. Being a part of the Internet can give meaning to a person's life.

• Ultimately, in a world of declining industrial production, the Internet represents an alternative future, another sense of life. The key words of this future are communication and freedom, interaction and journey, technology and unlimited possibility, virtual reality and ecology. "You have become a passenger on the space shuttle, my brother, and may no police ever interfere with our travels." In the Net there is more pleasure and money to be earned than in our former industries. "The Internet generation does not think that it will become a tool or be crushed in an industrial battle that overcomes it, but on the contrary, will be a pioneer of the first society of the imagination."[7]

─) The Place of the Church

First of all, the church must be "in." It is important for the Church to put on the Internet not only its doctrine, but above all—through sound, image, graphics, and interaction—the life-giving presence of Christ. For the Church *not* to be on the Internet would mean cutting itself off from the sense of history. It would deny its own spirit that is universal communion. By excluding itself from the Internet, the Church would show that, contrary to Christ, it refuses to give the world its body.

How must the Church show the presence of the Gospel on the Internet? It is obvious that in the first place the Church will use the services of the Internet for its research, its intercommunion, its teaching, and its internal administration. But what about evangelization? The Internet requires first of all that what we are, our possessions and our relationships, should be communicated: an open page, answering religious questions, giving spiritual help and a personalized presence to personal questions. Images, music, and singing make a community present. There is information that the official Church should convey to anyone who needs it: what the Church thinks about this or that controversial topic, how to prepare for baptism, and so on.

There are other services that should be the particular responsibility of every living community. There are thousands of personal services, like helping isolated persons, stories narrated for children by seniors and available online, relationships with people abroad, spiritual companionship for those who do not want to meet anyone in the flesh. Can Christians be active agents of the World Wide Web, especially through bringing some good news (some "good") to isolated, handicapped persons, locked in their problems? Would there not be a new breath to be given to religious congregations, to retired people? The Gospel is creating communion with this vision; the universal communion is the future, the Bible project.

The Need for a Ground of Silence and Desire

The presence of the Internet raises a basic question. In this huge empty electronic landscape containing all knowledge and multiple relationships, how will the way of Christ be perceived? What will make the "figure" spring up from the "ground"?

Formerly, children born in countries with a rich Christian tradition first met a powerful Church. At the high place in the village is the cathedral in the heart of the city with the bishop and the procession of priests. As they grew up children met the other masters at school and in the town hall. The family controlled the way these three figures were seen and interpreted.

In the media era, there are no longer three or four figures, but thousands. Children are born into a forest of figures: movie stars, sports heroes, singers, ads, punk hairstyles, and the latest electronic inventions. Moreover, the imaged and vibrant language of television, the Internet, and radio does not lead them to reflect but only to be tuned in according to the wants, the fashions, and the tastes of the moment. So the single figure that imposed itself on the consciousness by its social and historical weight does not exist anymore. Then why should Christ be selected? This is the basic question. It is the cause of our social failure in religious education. Our teaching today is only one figure among others. We would like to believe that we could solve the problem through better teaching methods. This is an illusion; there are too many figures, too many emotions throwing people off balance.

Do you want to evangelize? Begin by creating an expectation. Gandhi was successful because the crowds were thirsty for liberation. The disciples listened to Christ because they did not have an image of Christ. It is because the disciples had an internal longing for Christ that they could hear Christ. Wake up the longing that is dormant! Speak to those who are ready to listen.

Here silence is more determining than the word, because the outside word has some weight only if it meets the inner word, implicitly expectant. The Jews could not accept Jesus because they had drawn the shape and content of the future messiah too sharply. Silence, the expectation without precise content, the capability of being surprised is the condition of the Word of Another, as the blank page is the condition of the printed text.

How Can We Arouse This Expectation? Marketing teaches us that the first step consists in listening to the needs and evaluating them. Commerce teaches us that the quality of welcome in a store is the first condition of selling. The Christian answer is along the same line, and it is called the Incarnation. It is the persevering, personalized attention to the other that finally creates the expectation and the welcoming silence. In that sense, insofar as the Church on the Internet will start by listening and meet the deep needs, it will create the expectation that must precede any word.

Christian institutes of communication today must include "marketing and evangelization" in their program. These necessary programs will work only to the extent that they are in the Spirit of the Incarnation and Redemption.

Awakening Interiority Is the Key to a Deep Religious Communication The real solution to the multiplicity of words and images is in the awakening of interiority. Marcel Légaut states: "Only a faith built upon the awakening of interiority will be able to stand firmly in the world." A person who is being appealed to by thousands of figures and allurements, information, advertisements and new technologies chooses spontaneously according to immediate needs and superficial interests. One can choose the voice and truth of Christ only if one has been awakened previously to the taste of being one's self, really human and free. We lack the words here to name that basic experience of the birth of one's self. Some expressions are "awakening to one's self," "listening to one's intimate needs," "becoming conscious of one's inner and sacred mystery." Awakening interiority requires the ground of which I have spoken, but still more the encounter with awakeners, of witnesses rooted in their innermost being.

—) Questions for Reflection

1. What is your experience of change in the Church? How does the metaphor about Satan in this chapter resonate within you in regard to change?

2. What does it mean when we say that the "ground" is more important than the "figure"? Give an example.

3. Do you think that focusing on the "ground" is upsetting the Western Church? Why?

4. What does "modulation" have to do with communication? How can you use "modulation" in your evangelization and catechizing experiences?

5. Identify some steps we might take to educate our evangelizers, catechists, and Church leaders for understanding the importance of "ground" for our ministries.

6. "Only a faith built upon on the awakening of interiority will be able to stand firmly in the world." What does this statement mean to you?

CHAPTER 4

Toward Another Model of Communication

The main turning point of evangelization in the
twenty-first century will be this: it will
depend less on the proclamation of
our truths than on our ability to
turn ourselves toward others.
In conversation with others
the Gospel will appear.

Do we dare to speak of commerce when we are referring to evange-lization? In an article that I sent to about twenty religious people in ten countries, I proposed the model of commerce as a model of communication. My reasoning was based on the text in the Easter liturgy that speaks of the Incarnation as an "admirable commerce" between God and us. The Merriam Webster dictionary gives the first definition of commerce as "social intercourse: interchange of ideas, opinions, or sentiments." The reaction I received to the article, based on strictly using commerce in its mercantile sense, was definitely negative.

- "I have enormous difficulties associating evangelization to commerce even if it is helpful," writes Ligia Saniz, professor at Cochabamba University in Bolivia. "Commerce has strictly to do with making profits . . . this model does not fit the Church."

- Pierre Belanger, a Jesuit working in the media in Canada says, "One of my major criticisms of televangelists is the commercial character of their organization . . . for that reason I feel strongly reluctant to think of presenting the Gospel in terms of "buying" or "selling."

- Guy Marchessaut, a journalist responsible for the communication department at St. Paul's University in Ottawa, Canada, suggests that the word *exchange* be used instead of the word *commerce*.

- The same reluctance comes from the economist J. M. Albertini. "I don't think that the word *commerce* works in France . . . though it may be understood better in Anglo-Saxon countries."

- F. Kirupakaran, a wise man who is responsible for the Christian Center for Communication in Madras, India, writes, "I hope that this term means that we should shift from the model of teaching to a relational or transactional model."

- I received the same reaction from J. Eilers, specialist in social communications and misseology in the Philippines. "I agree with the idea but the word *commerce* is too marked. I propose the use of the term *convergence*. A communication is converging when the parties walk down a road and share (N. J. Eilers, in his treatise on communication).

—) **W**hy Use the Model of Commerce and the Internet?

If I want to use the term *commerce* to spread the faith, some may think that I am thinking of handing on the Gospel as a business. How can we help but recognize that some Christians and non-Christians have in the past and still today treat the Gospel as a business and some still do so today? We are not dealing here with that issue. We are not talking about selling the Gospel as merchandise. Nor do we think that to evangelize means that we are selling the Gospel, in the sense of evangelizing to make a profit nor even using the profits from such an endeavor in a more or less honest way. We are proposing that the faith be communicated according to models of communication other than those that were used in the past, teaching and proclaiming. What I am proposing is that we should use the two most predominant models of communication today. The first, commerce, is the most predominant model being used by the population as a whole. The second, the Internet, points to the future.

Must we abandon the term *commerce* for some term that seems to be more "pure"? The reader will decide. I propose the term, although I know that it may leave a bad taste in one's mouth. Why? I think that it expresses the most influential way of living in our time. Human psychology has been changing little by little under the influence of the media and the great number of diverse choices that people can make. In terms of influence, commerce is outstripping science, education, and the Church's authority. Indeed the people of Africa, like those of China and Brazil, are not even waiting for the big shopping malls to practice the mode of communication we call "commerce." They are already showing their genius in this matter. Never in the past has the idea of commerce controlled what was considered important in terms of values. It was the "well-read" intellectuals, politicians, or religious leaders who were the guides to living a good life. People did not discuss what their leaders said; they simply learned and obeyed.

In the culture I grew up in, I was taught that the primary value was God, the Truth, and that I must submit my life to this absolute, to the extent of sacrificing all my possessions. Then the world of commerce began to intrude. The world of commerce says *the first value is yourself*. It is the human being and the goods that are being produced that define humanity. Emmanuel Peteyron and Robert Salmon write the following about the sociocultural effects of the new technologies:

> The business corporation is capable of providing at an acceptable cost the needs of the consumer in order to satisfy his desires. This is the principal goal of American firms. Thanks to the new psychological tools that they use it is possible to know in real time the behavioral clues that show that product the individual is willing to buy. . . . The notion that happiness comes from consuming goods becomes fundamental.[1]

How does a "Christian" approach such realities? Christians find it easier to practice commerce then to think spirituality. In this time of the market economy, with its growing dependence on electronic technologies, the Church should integrate more clearly the values of commerce and marketing. In the past the Church has baptized the strategies of announcement, proclamation, teaching, work, and action. Isn't it time to "Christianize" commerce? How can people say that commerce is intrinsically a bad "activity," when the majority of the population, including religious priests and nuns in good positions, spend so much time in the marketplace? We cannot claim that we are ready to "integrate the Gospel into a new culture" if we ignore the system of relationships that the electronic media have brought about.

I speak here of commerce and the Internet. Although the Internet is to some extent a new language, the model of communication is basically the same. It provides a vast menu, the possibility of surfing according to personal needs and interests, then the possibility of an interactive dialogue with others and the exchange of goods. The essence of the Internet is exchange. In his book *Thinking Communication,* Dominique Wolton writes, "The Internet is the reverse of television, exchange has primacy over image. . . . It is the dream of a brotherly world, without borders, without hierarchy between the rich and the poor, of which the techniques of communication would somehow be the standard bearer."[2]

Electronic technologies did not invent the relationship between the buyer and the seller. They have generalized it, lit it up with images and sounds. They have made it scientific, egalitarian, and global. They have made it the predominant mode of human relationships. The "bar code" automatically allows the store manager to know what the customer likes or does not like. Ratings-control devices measure every hour what the audience is watching and what changes they are making. The Internet puts into everyone's reach the information and the secrets of "tuned-in" people. Television offers a multitude of channels for the viewer to "surf." All of this is determining the new culture of communications. It is only when we take into account the electronic resources being used in the market economy that we can understand the new vision of human relationships. The audiovisual, the networking of computers, the globalization of brands, advertising and marketing, testing and warranty service contracts, the demand for international technical aid and guarantees are now shaping communication in our world. I propose that we must acknowledge these cultural changes and by baptizing them make them our way of communicating the Gospel. It is not a matter of endorsing commerce, but Christianizing it.

Such "baptism" encompasses four operations:

taking into account
purifying (cleansing)
blessing
socializing

Taking into Account

Taking something into account means internalizing a reality that is there and cannot be discounted. More than ever in history, the market economy is promoting commercial activity. Taking into account means seeing this reality and understanding it. The first question is, how are we to understand the meaning of commerce? I define it here in its basic sense, the exchange of goods after a transaction. I would add that if we can speak of baptizing it, it is only from that fundamental sense, involving exchange, goods to be traded, and the transaction.

A pure exchange in commerce does not exist. Without even speaking of the individual lure of profit, every market is "embroiled" in cultural, national, ideological, and political demands. When we are taking commerce into account, we will always have to make reference to its anthropological origins. We must now make explicit those attitudes and operations that are the framework of most current commercial relations in countries where the market economy is practiced:

- Commerce is an action wherein the partners share complementary interests. I have something to give you; you have something to give me. Each of us is interested. That is a completely different attitude from saying, "I have the truth and I proclaim it to enrich you."

- Commerce takes place between two free and equal persons. No one is obliged to sell or to buy. Unlike the relationship between priests and the faithful, or between teachers and students, in a commercial relationship no one is superior to the other.

- Commercial acts offer a convention and guarantees: "Satisfaction guaranteed or your money back"; "Three Year Warranty." The buyer wants to make sure that he or she was not cheated and that the product will be replaced or repaired if it proves faulty.

- Commerce depends on the satisfaction of the population. The philosophy of marketing in its deepest sense characterizes that process.

  Assessing the needs of a given population

  Simulating those needs

  Adjusting production based on feedback from the population

  Shaping the product

  Organizing communication for distribution and sale

Some of the great traders are convinced of the possibilities of the new technologies of information. They present the commercial relationship as a personal, even spiritual, relationship. We should probably see this as an unconscious shifting of goodwill onto the machine, as one might do with a domestic pet. Nevertheless this point of view is not without interest. "The computer facilitates the need for human communication. This is how Nintendo markets their products."[3]

In perspective, commercial activity must:

- participate in research, essentially in the area of social usage. The organization will often measure human lifestyles and hopes.

- go beyond the model of mass consumption by fostering the notion of the person.[4]

Pateyron and Salmon conclude, "the real progress lies in the joint success between the human factor and the technological factor."[5]

Are we being naive? Perhaps. Nevertheless, the first move in the "baptism" process is to acknowledge what is here, not because it is necessarily better, but simply because it is here. The new technologies amplify the practice of commerce, alter its forms, and make it the predominant mode of communication. Can we take into account all of these characteristics? Can we trust the good intentions? Here what is required is a radical and permanent purification, because both people and the social operations they conduct are inextricably both good and polluted.

Purifying

Etymologically, baptizing means immersing.

Neither profit nor globalization should be allowed to destroy human dignity and justice. . . . People have come to condemn commerce itself because they see that the system in which we are immersed is unacceptable. The market economy can only be accepted if the human person, in its interiority, in community, in its identity with all of humanity, is found there. This means that human dignity can be found both within the market and on the surface. This is what should always be the condition of our dialogues and our business dealings.

The Church and the wise persons of this time have for the most part condemned the aberrations of the market economy. "Economic liberalism finds in the global extension of the techniques of communication its best ideological justification. That 'it works.' The Internet seems to be the epitome of that viewpoint—the liberal ideology of the 'free flow' of information and the abolition of regulations. What is supposed to represent the most radical innovation in the field of communication lives conversely at the heart of the economic interests of our time."[6]

The desire to please the audience requires particular attention. Thanks to digitalization it is possible to record, produce, and distribute material at prices a thousand times lower that those in the past. Thanks to fiberoptic networks and satellites the costs of communication are lower and lower. In this environment the readers and listeners are more important than the writers and producers. There is a strong temptation to follow the public's whims, all the more so because is seems to be the best way to "make money." Kierkegaard foresaw this when he denounced this trend in the nineteenth century, calling it the "dictatorship of the audience."

Are we going to follow the demands of the public? As a fundamental process of communication, yes, we will. In matters related to the approach of truth and values, no. We cannot apply the criteria of the shopping center to the Truth and the Good. The Truth and the Good with capital letters are not the children of the ratings system but of the reason and the Spirit. Quality is of a different nature than quantity, and that which is transcendent does not depend on numbers. The proverbs express the old wisdom, "In every mob of people, there are more feet than brains." Still more radical is the Armenian proverb, "To any one speaking the truth, give a horse so that he can escape after saying it." "Numbers alone are not always right, even if they result from a democratic choice," writes Wolton. "If legitimacy is granted to numbers alone, how can we avoid people lapsing in conformity or even dogmatism?"[7] The author goes on to recommend that the place where the public has its space be distinguished from "the place of normative organization within a hierarchy."

Jesus the rabbi viewed the questions of its truth and the Good from the viewpoint of a supernatural perspective, beyond the laws of marketing. For Jesus the truth is to be found in the heart of the poor. "I thank you, Father, . . . because you have hidden these things from the wise and the intelligent and have revealed them to infants" (Luke 10:21). Paulo Freire in Latin America has made this text a fundamental reference for his pedagogy of the oppressed. The rich know what is good for the body; the poor know what is good for the total development of the person. The real poor know the real goods. So the reference to the poor is not only a necessity of justice, but also a necessity to know the Truth and the Good. It is important, that the rich classes of society should go back from time to time to the basics (to the beginning) in order to be regenerated. According to the Christian spirit, a real marketing should not trust only the law of bigger numbers, but also the understanding and appreciation of the poor.

Blessing

In my opinion, the basic elements of the commercial or Internet process can apply fully to the communication of the Gospel. If, according to St. Irenaeus's formula, "the glory of God is Man fully alive," I would dare to say that moving to a commercial model and the Internet will make it possible to give more honor to God. Commerce and the Internet create the possibility for people to live more fully than when they live under the submission to authority. Dialogue is more human than subjugation.

Let us emphasize the following points.

In the Gospel evangelizing is first of all proposing "Goods," which can be summed up in the words "living fully." Goods include the healing of blindness, liberation from the evil that torments us, opening the prison in which this consumerist society has locked us up, reconciliation among people, and the promise of eternal life. This is what we must stress in this first stage of evangelization: healing, developing, liberating. The fundamental language of evangelization is the presentation of the truth, the dogmas and laws of the Christian faith, under the perspective of what is right and good. The biggest problem in applying marketing techniques is that it is easier to awaken the instinctive needs of material satisfaction, than it is to discern and arouse the awareness of deeper spiritual needs. Here a simple advertisement is not enough; a "commercial" with spiritual vision is needed. What is called for is a prophet who knows how to read and stimulate the deeper needs dormant in everyone. This is the central and most difficult point of a Gospel in the marketplace. When the audience is superficially satisfied with the products of society, how can their spiritual depths be aroused?

And what about the truth? When we remember that the effectiveness of the message depends on its acceptance by the audience, when we remember how Jesus Christ himself was misunderstood, can we not ask what the truth is? The danger is obvious. To neglect the truth in the long run cannot help but harm everyone. This is the ground for Rome's insistence that doctrine is important. Yet how can we forget the example of the Master? Jesus healed on days when it was against the law of the Sabbath. He found the need to do good, to save a life was beyond the boundaries of legal prescriptions (Mark 3:1–6). Jesus narrated charming parables that could not be understood (Matthew 13:13). He performed many miracles that were misinterpreted. "You are looking for me not because you saw signs, but because you had all the bread you wanted to eat" (John 6:26).

Secondly, the starting point of evangelization will not be teaching, but experience. As in the Gospel of John, we will communicate what we have seen and touched. By becoming the "way" in our turn, we will enable others to touch and see. The audiovisual generation will believe only what it has experienced. Come and see, come and taste. This is the starting point of evangelization.

Ultimately, even if there are difficulties, evangelization will appear not as a whole to be swallowed, but as a long *process* of exchange, of human relationships, of services and guarantees. It will include the process of spiritual experience and of relations with other Christians. It will be a process of meeting mutual needs and accepting mutual contributions. The Easter liturgy speaks of the Incarnation as an "admirable commerce" between God and man. The process of evangelization shows a social concern for the poor. Are they not the ones who will be able to recognize the values and truths dwelling in their hearts even more than the rich? Are they not capable of receiving something essential from children, from the sick, from prisoners? These are serious questions that shake up the attitudes of an evangelizer who thinks that he is the "master of truth."

Socializing

In the Christian tradition, baptism integrates a person into the Church. We, of course, are not going to demand from nonbelievers with whom we meet in dialogue that they become members of the community of believers. Yet it is imperative that a sense of community is built up in the course of the dialogue. In the world of commerce, community might be called a network, club, or group. Many airlines have "advantage" cards that offer special services to their regular customers. We cannot turn on our computers without seeing the trademark for the software or listening to their commercial jingle. In the Catholic Church the sacraments are indelible signs of God's grace, not unlike a brand name or logo.

Simply imitating the ways of commerce is not the point. But we must understand that dialogue requires some sort of community among the participants even if they have diametrically opposed views. No dialogue involving the Gospel can take place without a minimum of human brotherhood, the beginning of a community, be it a meal, a party, a song, or a banner. At the great Eucharistic congress at Kuala Lumpur, the organizers sold inexpensive T-shirts. These were especially noticeable on the young Muslims who attended Mass in the public square. Their participation was not, of course, Eucharistic communion, but was it not a step toward communion? Dialogue requires somehow getting together with another. It is not possible to create dialogue without first shaking hands, without some physical contact, without taking the first steps to community.

The Socialization of the Global Village The global village is the particular way in which people are being socialized in our time. Marshall McLuhan invented the phrase "global village." Even though the use of the phrase has been criticized, I think that it is an image that is perfectly fitting, especially in these days of the Internet. It is a dangerous, even ambiguous image, but a truthful one that brings hope. "It is the well-known theme of the global village, of a world at an end, defeated by the techniques of communication. It is a foreshadowing of a world dominated by the values of communication. . . . The global village is the best support for economic liberalism, in that it crosses all the borders and presents a marketplace cleared of useless, nationalistic rules.[8]

We have to understand the meaning of the image as such. The meaning of the image of the global village must be distinguished from its development in myth. The global village does not refer to a world that might be achieved through superior technology. If you have ever lived in a village, you know about the kind of communication we are speaking of. The communication in the village is a communication of communion as opposed to the fast transmission of soon-to-be-forgotten stories and news. When a doctor entered the village, within five minutes everyone would know it, some of them in their pain, some in their joy. It is what they used to call the "Arabic phone." It is this Arabic phone that is being replaced by electronic communications, making the world a global village. But the Arabic phone never prevented the gap between the rich and the poor, hatred or killings, or clan secrets. The global village is like a pincushion on a magnet. The magnet is the common denominator orienting the pins and determining the space between them, just as in the past the land and the traditions of the village determined the relations between the people. As for the "values of communication," it is naive to believe that all people belong to a single village. There are lines of communication in the world in the sense that situations and technologies create special lines of sensibility, and specific orientations in the spirit. The lines of communication produced by the nature of a village differ from those produced by electronics. That is all I can say.

As for real communication, it is of a different nature; it is spiritual, transcendent, and intangible. For many people, unsatisfied with the anonymity and hectic pace of urban civilization, the global village has come to mean an idyllic land of peace and harmonious relationships. Wolton rightly denounces these fanciful dreams about the global village. How naive it is of us to believe that electronic communications can fix the communication problems in the world. The reality is not so simple. We have to instead look at the realistic hopes for such a village such as those we can find in *Redemptoris Missio* and *Aetatis Novae.*

Here is how I propose we conceive a global village

- It is made up of electronic technologies, waves and modulations that cross geographic and political borders. Little by little, the old borders become obsolete, creating a new state of mind in the population, changing the ways people travel, opening up the world. This creates a situation in which many will fear the loss of their identities and values. I call that the "gradient" of the mind and sensitivity.

- The gradient created by electronic surroundings will meet quite naturally with some populations in search of progress. This is particularly true of the younger generations in search of a future. Then the electronic gradient and the gradient of progress combine. We go from a 5 percent angle to a 10 percent angle. This combination will transform the idea of a global village, gathering together a theme for a whole generation who are more or less disappointed with the past and in search of an alternative future. Intuitively, and in a confused way, young people can make the Internet an instrument for the future. To these young people the Internet seems to be the tool and standard bearer to another way of living. They see it as bringing them happiness, freeing them from the weights of the industrial world and consumerism. They sense a new way of living, which is now being expressed in music, knowledge, and exchange of services, journeys, and global communication.

From this descriptive image we have passed to a mobilizing theme with its cloud of dreams and confusion. Is it Christian? We still have to add the "gradient" of biblical faith. We are moving to a world of unity and universal communion, toward "a new heaven and a new earth" (Revelation 21:1), in which all are reconciled with God, on earth and in heaven (see Colossians 1:19–20).

Young people today are insecure as they witness the decline of the industrial world. With their sensitivity to the opportunities presented in the technical and symbolic world of the media, we can hope to offer a future based in the global village. But as Christian educators and communicators we are not in a position to promise or secure anything. We can announce the possibility of another future, a future faithful to God's plan. But we can do so only if we are realistic about the possibilities of the global village. This can happen only if it is based on the prospect of real communication among peoples. We can say that there are reasonable expectations that this community will be created and enhanced by the new and promising technical instruments. This is a future that does not have to be distracted by the false promises of consumerism, but offers the happiness of interactive knowledge, of exchange of services and freedom to travel. Since McLuhan's time the concept of the global village has changed. From McLuhan's accurate description of the developing world of communication, the idea of the global village has become a dream and a call. As long as we are aware of that, why should we take away its poetic character?

With the help of the new technologies and the power of the Spirit, evangelization can be called to build up a certain kind of global village. Lamenting the misfortunes of the outcasts and the unemployed will have no effect if there is no call to build a future. How can the evangelizer help but find in the Bible the light and breath needed to speak to the global village? What greater example can there be to begin considering the implications of the global village than that of Abraham, the traveler?

─) **O**ur Definition of Evangelization

Sr. Angela Ann Zukowski and I have arrived at a definition of evangelization that integrates the most characteristic elements of the "new culture." Evangelization is "a conversation on the world's marketplace to exchange spiritual goods."

A Conversation

Sister Angela Ann proposes the word *conversation*. I was at first reluctant to accept it. In French the term takes on the meaning of common chatting, of discussion during a meal, of exchange of news in the marketplace. Consulting dictionaries, however, I noticed that the primitive meaning of the word *conversation* comes from the Latin *conversari*, which frequently means not "discussing" but "staying with," "living somewhere." Related to it we find *conversus, convergere,* which is "turning" or "bending." In the same line in the dictionary we find "lay brother" and "conversion." These terms are extremely strong. Beyond the meaning of a simple exchange of words, they point to a movement of a person's deepest being. They include the foundation of dialogue, the capability of putting one's self into the point of view of the other. I might well replace the word *conversation* with the term "mutual conversion." But we will keep the word *conversation,* understood in terms of its basic etymological meaning. This shows that evangelization does not demand automatic and instant radical change.

What is the first act of conversation? It is a *turning point,* a way of seeing and being there, an effort to move one's self off center, to put one's self in the place of the other. Communication with the other does not begin with thinking about the best way to put one's message across. It begins with a sympathetic, even prophetic, look at reality. The greatest danger, and the fault of many evangelizers and politicians, is that they seek first of all to get to an audience and persuade it of their own point of view. They are not ready to listen to their audience. They do not feel the call of the people in themselves. They also do not use the filter of the Gospel to perceive the depth of the call underneath the surface turmoil. All too often their concern is, "How should I act so that my image and my message might get through?"

I do not see how those who want to spread the faith can have a deep sense of their audience without an ongoing contemplation, in cooperation with the Holy Spirit, of the reality of the human condition and the circumstances in which people live. The intellectual approach using sociological themes can help, but it is necessary to go much deeper. Evangelizers must become immersed in human reality and feel the deeper void hidden beneath the rebellion and suffering.

They must even be sensitive to the needs that are addressed in the advertisements found on TV and radio and in newspapers. The basic issue is the way we manifest ourselves in our society and culture.

Once we have truly seen the other, we are ourselves able to utter the silent cry of the people to which we belong. We have to be clear here; the cry rises up in us. The word we share springs from the depths of our own being, rather than from some prepackaged theological doctrine. Then the proverb will apply, "When a sheep is bleating in the sheepfold, the whole flock knows that it is thirsty."

From my viewpoint, the main turning point for evangelization in the twenty-first century will be this: it will depend less on the proclamation of our truths than on our ability to turn ourselves toward others. In conversation with others, the Gospel will appear.

In the World's Marketplace

In the past missionaries left their own countries to live in a local situation, incarnating the message with unbelievable heroism. Today the situation of the global village calls every Christian to be a missionary in a new way, to leave one's country while remaining in one's land. This is a worldwide type of incarnation. How can we bring this about? In a threefold way

- By letting down our own barriers and forcing ourselves to feel "worldwide." The orientation of the great Christian missionary journals is remarkable from that viewpoint. (Note: Some French journals like *l'Actualité Religieuse,* the religious news, have definitely turned toward the worldwide dimension and being open to different religions and cultures.) Poverty and presence in one's own neighborhood should not be used as a pretext to stay within one's walls. The poor were the first to adopt radio, television, and, sometimes, new means of transportation. We must remember the expatriates and the crowded trains in Africa or India.

- By frequently including in our conversation other cultures and religions. We must refuse to be locked into our daily audience, even if they are our own parishioners. Meeting the concrete needs of our listeners is a priority. We cannot think that this stance is a historical deviation, a misinterpretation of the Bible. Today it is not a question of pouring out the news of the world to the audience. As Pope John XXIII said, "the whole world is my family." I am in the world, and all the religious of the world are in me as I speak. As we do with the computer, we speak from a large database in which everyone is invited to tune in according to his or her own interests.

• Ultimately, people want to be initiated into modern technologies in order to be in the "in-group," to speak the language of this time. And this is the language that is crossing all the borders of the world. When we form people, for example if we train Africans in social and religious communications, it cannot be simply to make them use the *Catechism of the Catholic Church,* although that is an important part of their formation. First they must be trained so that the Church in their country speaks the language that their people understand. Moreover these new evangelizers should be pioneers in bringing that language to the future.

Sharing Our Spiritual Goods

For centuries, faith has been presented mostly as doctrine, as intellectual content. This has been so because we were in a predominantly print and written medium ruled by academics. To this generation we will present it under the aspect of the good *(sub specie boni).*

In Indonesia, as we started sharing sessions between audiovisual producers of different religions—Buddhists, Christians, Hindus, and Muslims—we asked ourselves, how can we dialogue with one another in a way that is mutually stimulating? What is our purpose? What will result in the greatest good of the country, for our local communities?[9] The answer was clear: we could not begin by sharing our beliefs and dogmas. We had to share that which we had in common: how we live, what things we have, and our religious sensitivities. We decided that sharing our goods before our ideas was where we had to begin our intercultural and interreligious dialogue. This is also the best and oldest way to bring the Gospel to the marketplace.

Bill Gates is not our master of communication. But by writing *The Road Ahead*[10] he prompted us to seek how we can continue to proclaim the Gospel now and in the future.

What about the criticism that we are going too much with the stream of events? There are two ways that one can go in a current. One can either fight one's way upstream or make too much use of the current. Perhaps we are trying to go faster than current thinking by trying to integrate the process of commerce into the communication of the Gospel. It is up to the reader to discuss and judge this strategy.

The question as to whether we use or reject the term *commerce* remains. We must, however, use the fundamental concepts that make up commerce: exchange, goods, negotiation, and dialogue.

—) Questions for Reflection

1. How do you feel about applying the term *commerce* to the Church's evangelization efforts?

2. Is the concept of Christian commerce a reasonable one?

3. Does the word *conversation* have the same connotation for you as described in this chapter?

4. How might a new understanding of the "conversation concept" enhance your ministry and the ministry of the Church?

5. How would you interpret the "new missionary" role for the Church today in the new media culture? How can we prepare women and men in ministry for this new role?

CHAPTER 5

The Body Is the Message

It is up to us as medium to continue that message of Christ!

What is the message of Christ? The usual answer is "love one another," or some maxim of the Gospel. The message consists of what Christ said as found in the Scriptures and codified in the doctrine of the Church. A female student of communications in the Catholic center of formation in Dallas, Texas, asked her director, "Which message are all these techniques for?" To her surprise he answered, "The message? It is clearly stated in the Catechism, in what the Pope says, in the rosary."

This is the biggest misunderstanding between the generation of the book and that of television. One is a literary and the other is an audiovisual culture. In the academic literary culture where theology is studied, the message is perceived primarily as words. Is this the way the children of television and rock music understand the message? The newspaper *Libération* reported on the annual Love Parade in Berlin. Over one million young people participated in the parade in July 1997. The paper reported "The participant in the love parade goes where the sound will make him resonate the most. . . . These 'vibes' of insistent music. . . . A 'rave' cannot be told, but lived. With the noise, the participant expresses himself in a bodily way."[1]

My point here is that the message of Christ is primarily in what he did, not what he said. What was true in the time of Jesus is even truer today. In the audiovisual world large parts of the population live impregnated with electronic sounds and images. As evangelizers, it is up to us as medium to continue that message of Christ!

──) **W**here Is the Message in Today's Culture?

In the sixties, Dom Helder Camara, bishop of Recife, Brazil, spoke for a few minutes on Swiss television. I do not remember what he had to say. I only remember his thin face, his bright eyes, his hands lifted up in the air like a snake. These images were loaded with significance and have never left me. It sparked something that lay in me waiting to be awakened. I never forgot the message behind the words: "Never forget the poor."

In audiovisual terms, the message is produced by the effect it has on you. It is an effect first communicated by images, gestures, vibrations, and history. The message in audiovisual terms does not operate on the level of conceptual intelligence but in the nervous system. Publicist Jacques Séguéla gives this advice to television performers. "You will be judged more by your face than by your brain. . . . Every moment you must witness to your passion."

The last four commandments Séguéla gives to people in communication are:

  7. Be a name not an ideology.

  8. Learn to become a star.

  9. Promise hope, not a program.

  10. Become what you are.[2]

──) **U**nion with the Body

How can Christians declare their message in the world today where what is said only counts for 7 percent of what people learn?[3] Cardinal Martini in his pastoral letter about communication begins his reflection by commenting the episode of the sick woman healed by touching Jesus' garment from behind. Communicating in a mediatic way operates by somehow touching the body, or a person's garment as an extension of the body. Jesus' healing "power" travels through the garment.

In an interview Cardinal Martini explains, "There is [in the Church] a way of speaking that belongs to the last four or five centuries. It has a tendency towards intellectualism. This kind of drift towards abstraction did not exist in the primitive Church or the Bible. There the modes of communication were more lively and concrete. God is presented in what he does. In the sixth century catechisms they began to speak in terms of abstract truths. . . . I think that we have a great opportunity with these new means of communication to remind ourselves that the Gospel is above all narration and presentation of how God lives. . . . I think we should really change our language . . . [to] a language of communication from heart to heart, a language of emotional vibration."[4]

"The body is the message" is not simply a stylistic device or a striking formula. It is the reality of the message from the culture of the media. Saying "the body of Christ" is only giving a Christian name to the term we find in the medium. As Regis Debray writes about the famous phrase "the medium is the message," "Our great wise man is not McLuhan but St. John." "The Word was made flesh" could be translated perfectly by "The Word was made medium." Here body, flesh, and medium are equivalent terms. "Such is the power of the Incarnation making the ambiguous person of Christ the most powerful king ever at the disposal of a religion to conquer the earth."[5] It is precisely the genius of McLuhan to have somehow resuscitated a very old philosophy. What leads the world is not the ideas but the media, what St. John calls "the flesh." Is it a scandal? Yes, for anyone who remains locked in abstract intellectual patterns. Yes, for anyone who conceives the body simply as a part of a human being, and the media simply as a means to deliver content. In the culture of the media the body (consequently the medium) is our way to have a soul and to communicate it. In the dimension of the space and time of the soul, the body is not a wheelbarrow carrying content, but a way of being in the world and of having the world.

When I asked Marshall McLuhan what he meant by content, he answered me in a very direct way. "You are the content! The content of the Bible is not the ideas. When you read the Bible, you tune into it, you become the medium. You are the message."

Reading the Gospels this way helps us to comprehend them better. When Christ says, "This is my body, take and eat," he is expressing the very heart of his message and his language is perfectly "tele-visual."

Nothing has helped me to interpret the Gospel as much as watching Michael Jackson's musical tours on television. Like the disciples in

Jesus' time I was scandalized by the violence of some of Jesus' words. "Unless you eat the flesh of the Son of Man and drink his blood, you have no life in you" (John 6:53). According to an intellectual interpretation we can read these words as a metaphor to mean that we must totally obey the doctrine of the Master. By seeing the relationship of the performers to their public, we perceive a different reality. It means to "make one body with." The first sense of the word disciple is "to walk behind." But by seeing the relationship of popular singers with their public, we now see it in a different light. To be a *disciple* means to "make one body with," in the first sense of the word, which is to walk behind. Michael Jackson's fans copy his gestures, his style of walking, and his clothes. They become his disciples. Comprehending the Gospel is not primarily an intellectual process. Comprehending means making one's body with, participating, resonating with the same vibrations.

The message then consists of belonging to the network, to the "Net," or to the body.

We understand nothing about the Internet if we do not perceive that, for this generation, intellectual content does not matter as much as belonging to the vehicle, the World Wide Web. De Kerkhove is right, "the connected intelligence" is more important than the fruit of the shared intelligence. In biblical terms we say "belonging to the body," becoming "one body with." Both the media and the Bible use the same language and, underneath, the same philosophy, one that is committed, physical, sensorial, linked to a group. Understanding is participating.

Table 1 summarizes the way the different cultures are reflected in the three ways of evangelization.

—) The Body and the Words

We should understand that the body is, of course, the physical appearance revealing the person. It is also everything that is linked to the body—its scars, family, friends, the community, the political party, house, garden, car, bank account, the diplomas that one receives, and the media. In Christian terms it would also mean the Church, the "Mystical Body" of Christ, the communities eating the Eucharistic Bread in memory of the Lord.

TABLE 1 Three Cultures, Three Ways of Evangelizing

	The Age of Oral Culture, the Beginning of the Church	The Age of Print Sixteenth to Twentieth Centuries	The Electronic Age, the Era of the Media— the End of the Twentieth Century
Predominant Medium	The spoken word	The book	The media
The Transmitter	The herald The proclaimer The preacher The witness The performer of miracles	The teacher The preacher The writer The explainer The demonstrator	Immersion in the media The author Being dialogue Fashioning of one's own image The programmer
The Message	Narrative Prophesy Testimony Miracles	Words Doctrines Catechisms Theology	The media itself The body Technology Communication
The Receivers	Listeners The converted Those becoming disciples Those being baptized Members of the community	Learners Memorizers Understanders Practitioners Doers	Those who resonate Those who choose Those who are online Those who are connected Those who belong
Social Structure	Community Disciple	Parish School (Catechetical)	Communities of like-minded people The marketplace

What about words, speech? It would be wrong to say that words count for nothing! They are always here forming a union with the body. They are no longer the vanguard and impulse of the message, but only its fortress. His Excellency the Word, enthroned in catechism classes, is now replaced by the media, His Excellency the Body. The issue between the word and the body is not that of one being present and the other absent, but that of rank.

Radio speaks to the imagination. It is like receiving a thousand postcards. Therefore, when awakening the imagination, hearing the tone of voice, the style, the delivery, and above all the rhythm are essential. Conviction and love can be perceived "by ear." More important than the words is the resonance of the voice.

We speak of a style of radio. In a survey on Christian radio conducted in France, the first quality stressed by the listeners is the warm character of the radio (93 percent). Then comes enrichment (84 percent), dynamism (80 percent), credibility (79 percent), character, etc.[6] Where are the words?

The words are inside the voice, demanded by the voice, but no longer brought by the voice. The breath of a lover causes him to say the words "I love you." If the lover loves no longer, he can say the same words, but the tone is not the same and at once the beloved will hear the difference. Words are essential, but the message is elsewhere. Even if one is a good actor, sooner or later his voice and the muscles tensing in his face will reveal him for the liar he is. It is pity we do not have a recording of the voice of Jesus, for we would probably understand the Gospel differently.

—) **W**ill the Truth Suffer?

The truth may suffer if we lose too much from the fortress of words. Yet the truth is not reduced to doctrinal formulas. We will gain in that other aspect of truth that is the spiritual knowledge of a personal relationship with Christ. This is how the faith was first communicated in the beginning of Christianity.

Table 2 shows the advantages and limitations of written and audiovisual communication and the messages they communicate.

—) **W**hich Style of Teaching?

Nothing will replace teaching, which is elaboration, explanation, and transmission. Someone has written, "Faith is not a cry." But should it necessarily be abstract and rationally logical? Teaching the faith cannot be reduced to repeating the *Catechism*. Since St. Augustine's *De catechizandis rudibus (First Catechetical Instruction)*, we are invited to a more historical, symbolic, and liturgical form of catechesis.

For the people in the era of the media, we should embrace the following:

- To begin with, they place their values in interesting people and in pleasure. They like meeting important people, having spiri-

TABLE 2 The Message in Two Cultures

Writing	Audiovisual
The doctrine is the message.	The way the image affects you is the message.
The message is in the words.	The message is in the modulation of images and in their "coming and seeing."
My students listen to me speaking.	My sheep hear my voice.
The message is found by studying the text (scholastic theology).	The message is found by belonging to the body (Internet).
In the last few centuries, there is little information and it is transmitted by writing and word of mouth. The good formation is rooted and structured.	"The child who arrives in school today has watched television and played video games for a long time. The way he receives information is not structured, and images play a very important role in his life. Therefore there has been little appeal to his reasoning powers. For this reason, his spatial temporal perceptions are not always precise."[7]

tual experiences in high places, going on pilgrimages, and celebrating feasts. This also involves emotional praying, spoken testimonies, music and song, readings, films and images. It helps create an atmosphere of freedom and exchange in warm spiritual experiences. At this stage, key words and biblical sentences may emerge.

- Secondly, people will need to discover ways to deepen the spiritual experience. They can discuss the experience with friends, with a spiritual director, or even better, with the symbolic person who introduced them to the experience. People will try to relive the first experience, searching for a suitable atmosphere through music, spiritual and biblical reading, or listening to Christian radio.

- The third stage is biblical deepening. While the previous generation would go to catechism classes, this generation goes to Bible study, but with those teachers who can revive and reanimate stories of the great biblical figures. Christianity will be taught in a symbolic way, helping people to identify with Moses or Jesus in whom they discover the fulfillment of their most secret dreams and a revelation of how they should live their lives.

- In the next stage, there is a mix of theological systemization and the study of spirituality. These subjects are best taught historically with suggestions for ways they can be applied to spiritual development today. At this stage, many people dedicate themselves to catechetical activities with children and young people. These last two stages are effective only when they take place in conjunction with an activity in and for the Church.

- The last stage includes more systematic and critical biblical study. I have not mentioned the development of people within their parishes or through social relationships. Although these are important, they are not really new. After a period of evangelization it appears more and more difficult to define a typical Christian formation from the point of view of the institution. Modern technologies give priority to connections and choices, being plugged in, pointing and clicking.

In a multimedia world the issue is not abolishing books or courses. Multimedia is not the image of the written word alone, but the images of both, the spoken and written word. The Internet and the CD-ROM do not lead us away from writing; they integrate it. The audiovisual is now predominant, a predominance we have to respect. But we cannot exclude the word in the name of the audiovisual; that would be walking on one foot. The culture does not exclude the literary and oral word, but animates it.

I would dare to give the following advice. If, as we have argued in these pages, being medium is the most important thing, let us take the style and media suiting the best we have to offer and most likely to strengthen us as medium. We agree that we should learn new technologies; we have to develop to the maximum our capabilities of personal extension through technology. We have to attend the seminars and workshops that make it so. Yet after a period of initiation, we have to adopt those technologies that best fit our personality and talents. It may be the Internet, a diagram on paper, the spoken or written word, or creating audiovisual montages. When we want to do our best, we have to take our particular audience into account. What helps us to give the best of ourselves by communicating? The first thing we have to pay attention to is not what techniques we are planning to use, but how we are connected with the Source and our personal vocation.

The body is the message. Is this purely a sheer theological consideration? I think the pastoral considerations will cause a pastoral upheaval similar to that which happened after the invention of printing. Let's look at a few of the issues:

- The message is more in what you are than in what you say. It is the priority of the spiritual over the intellect. We have to renew the style and programs of our formation institutes. It is not enough to learn how to think and speak rightly; we must also learn to have the right voice and the transparent face of God's Spirit.

- You speak through your *aura,* that is, through the radiation of your personality. But you also speak through your relationships and the substructure linked to you. Relationships and organization are not first in evangelization, your body is. Thinking without organization is like thinking without a body. To the younger generation the laws of modern management and the conditions of marketing should be taught as a necessity of the body, not simply as a means of utilizing it.

- Building the Church means primarily building a *network.* Before establishing anything, before launching a Christian radio station, create the network. Do not buy anything; do not build a permanent structure if it is not in connection with developing a network. Insist on formation; it is first of all through formation that a person takes shape.

- In order to be present "as a body" to this world, especially in the media, the Church has to be concerned about creating *events.* A great example of this is the thorough and technical preparation surrounding the pope's journeys. We exist to serve the population by actions, by celebrations and feasts, by taking a stand that echoes the Gospel. "All you need to say is 'yes' if you mean 'yes,' and 'no' if you mean no" (Matthew 5:37).

- In the era of the media, the leader-group pairing is the basic structure of evangelization. Charisma is the inspirited center. In evangelization as in politics, the charismatic leaders and the communities linked to them are essential. In these communities the breath and body are one. If the Church wants to evangelize, it will have to promote charisma and prophecy. A body in which the administrative and official structures are too predominant does not facilitate evangelization.

- In missionary activity, the first concern will be to become one in body with the population. The best evangelization will be achieved through mixing with people, not through the word descending from above. To this end, diocesan and missionary centers should gather religious professionals in journalism and the media, and also those who work in secular society, to make one body. Special attention should be paid to the Vatican document *Aetatis Novae*.

—) Consequences for Communication

If the body is the message—that is the total body, united in community through electronics—then our patterns of communication must be modified. I think that the usual descriptions of communication, made mostly by sociologists, badly express the mediatic message. Their viewpoints come from the schools and sometimes from journalism. What matters for them is the transmission of intellectual content, in an understandable form, with a social impact that can be evaluated.

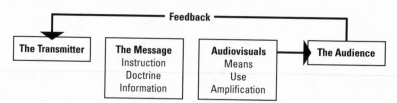

The practice of media communication, such as the understanding of evangelical communication, leads us to another diagram.

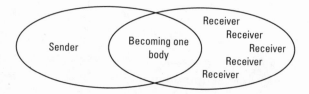

Here the communication is from body to body. It is more akin to conjugal love than to school. It is a conveyance of "affects," of sensitivities and imagination, of intuition and moves rather than ideas. The first communication is measured in understanding, the second in participation. The first leads to a doctoral thesis, the second to a religious or political group. The first apostles understood it rightly. Body-to-body communication means being baptized and becoming "one body" in Christ. No one better than Saint John defines that sensual audiovisual transmission aiming at communion. "We declare to you what was from the beginning, what we have heard, what we have seen with our eyes, what we have looked at and touched with our hands, concerning the word of life—this life was revealed, and we have seen it and testify to it. We declare to you what we have seen and heard so that you also may have fellowship with us" (1 John 1:1–3).

──) **A** Different Emphasis

Such is the secret call of the culture of the media, bringing about what you say with your life, "This is my body given for you." In France, a priest gave a good image of what we are trying to say here. The Abbé Pierre was elected by an overwhelming majority as the most popular man in our country. This courageous old man, with an emotional and crude language, showed a face akin to that of Jesus in the Gospel. He was speaking with a "given body," a body crying, getting angry, performing miracles for the homeless people. Receiving his message consisted of making one body with that body.

What we are proposing here is not a replacement, but a shifting of emphasis in the pastoral work, going back to the language of the Gospel and the early years of the Church.

──) **Q**uestions for Reflection

1. "It is up to us as a medium to continue that message of Christ." What does that mean for you? For your faith community?

2. What is the difference between the way those in the early church communicated what they believed and how we communicate today? What can we learn from this reflection?

3. What dynamics or approaches are used to attract youth in our culture today? Is there something we can learn for our own evangelization and catechizing ministries?

4. How do you awaken the imagination of the people you minister to?

5. What new catechetical approaches can you identify that can relate to the message of this chapter?

Reactivate Paul Beyond the Walls

From now on, the church is no longer a big
building dominating a city, it is only a
simple pavilion in the great field of
the international trade fair.
—THE BISHOP OF REIMS

St. Peter's in Rome and St. Paul's Beyond the Walls, two basilicas, one
in the Vatican at the heart of the city, the other outside the walls of
Rome, are not only an old symbol, but also an expression of the conditions of the Gospel. Peter is the rock, the guardian of the original
roots, sometimes uncompromising. Paul has been sent among the
pagans, called not to baptize but to evangelize (1 Corinthians 1:17).
Here are two currents, two ways of being Christian and continuing
the presence of Christ.

There is no question of ascribing the task of mission to Paul
alone. Peter and Paul are entrusted with spreading the Gospel in different ways. My opinion is that in the era of the media we have an
urgent need of Paul, of the Paul with the audacity to climb up to the
Areopagus, the meeting place. Moreover I think that this era of the
media tearing down the old borders offers to the Church a particular
opportunity to renew its missionary spirit and organization. We have
not only to accept the differences between Peter and Paul but also to
look at them in a positive way. I propose here to revive the spirit of
Paul in the Church. Why?

──) **T**he Church as a Simple Pavilion

If we must reactivate Paul's spirit, it is primarily because the world of modern communications has materially and definitively put the Church in a missionary situation. Electronics have put the Church organically in a situation of "diaspora" (scattering) and made it one channel of influence among others. The predominance of Christianity is over. So is the practice of evaluating the Church by the number of stone buildings and the number of participants in Sunday worship. Through the media, through the Internet, the Church is put in a position of becoming the salt of the earth, scattered and broken down to give taste. More than ever, the mission is specialized. It has moved from call to situation.

"From now on, the church is no longer a big building dominating a city, it is only a simple pavilion in the great field of the international trade fair." That formula comes from the bishop of Reims, then rector of Lyons Catholic University, both sociologist and theologian.[1]

I can create no better image that seizes upon the situation of the Church in the global village made by modern electronic technologies. Yesterday, at the heart of the village, the church was the highest building. Growing up under its shadow, a little child could not escape its prestige. The steeple rising toward the sky extended the raised finger of teachers and parents. "Be attentive, that is what you have to do, there is the truth, here you find heaven's direction." When we used to come with a youth group to a little village in Corsica, the parish priest at the Sunday high Mass started his sermon by telling us, "On behalf of the village, I welcome you." The pastor indeed was not the mayor, but he appointed himself the village's representative. It is not so long ago when the religious marriage was more important, if not more legal, than the civil wedding. In many places, this has collapsed or is radically breaking down. A new image is rising, that of St. Patrick's Cathedral, an erstwhile grand building crushed between the skyscrapers in New York. In the largest cities of Africa, Latin America, and Asia the majesty of the great religious buildings is giving room today to the great hotels, banks, palaces, and museums.

In the eyes of the world, the Church is valued not for its temporal powers, but by its capacity to meet the expectations of the audience. The erosion of the psychological and moral power of the Churches over the human spirit is more subtle and deeper than the ending of its temporal powers. Even for the old countries of the Christian tradition, the Church is no longer The Voice, but one voice. It is no longer "the" salt of the earth, but one salt. Everyone has a choice.

──) ▲ Traveling Church

Electronic technology, by multiplying communications and making them worldwide, forces the Church to take a journey. Here we are now associated with Paul the traveler, Paul going everywhere, daring everything, discussing with everyone. The major institutionalization of the Church dates back to the early days of printing, when, in order to fight against the Protestant Reformation, it surrounded itself with high walls of doctrine. This was the time of rigorous education of priests in seminaries, the formulization of doctrine in the catechism, the establishment of parochial schools. The Church at that time succeeded in becoming a solid presence firmly planted in the ground, attracting the faithful to itself. They would go to Church where the truth was.

In the culture of the media, the Church will indeed remain a place of reference and of pilgrimage. Nevertheless it will have to broadly reverse its centralizing tendencies and go out into the street, into the world. Belonging to the human caravan today no longer means being incarnated into the traditions of the village or the clan. It is "surfing," that is, running on the waves of the world, not only on the Internet but also on the radio, in the car, and on innumerable organized trips. Today the Church must ask questions and speak without waiting for the people to ask. We don't want to destroy the pastoral activity of the traditional parish church, but let us add to the list some pastoral work of presence on the waves, in multiple associations, in the groups and movements that build up society.

In May 1996, I met Alain Merieux, director of the first worldwide firm for vaccine production. Besides being a prestigious personality in the Rhone-Alps region, he is president of the General Council and as such he exercises power over the management of public funds. As I requested some help for our center for research and promotion of religious communication, highlighting the international character of our impact, he answered me, "No doubt you can bring much to the region, but it is absolutely impossible for me to release a part of the budget for a center concerned with evangelization." After he thought about it for a while, he corrected himself and added, "If you organized a symposium with the archbishop, responsible Protestant leadership, the great mufti, the leading rabbi, to put together the best means to solve impossible problems for this city, delinquency, drug, violence in the suburbs, then we would give . . ." In my opinion, this man summed up in a simple proposition some characteristics of the evangelization for our time. Get together, put ourselves to the service of the great needs of the society, and speak up—but along with the others.

Yesterday Paul, like our first missionaries, used to travel by boat. That old mode of transportation explodes today in a thousand ways. Travel, my friends, travel! By phone and fax, by books and bulletins, by radio and the Internet. The mission of the Church has been successful for the last five centuries thanks to geographic institutionalization; let us now achieve it by being nomads.

How could we not rejoice with the majority of Catholics about the existence of the Vatican? It is there in our hearts, a place of coordination, a place to support Christians in trouble, a place distributing back the goods to the poorest of churches, a place for great celebrations. May the Vatican go even more deeply into its mission. But if we listen to the pleas of the new culture as recalled above, we also wish that the official Church existed differently, as one voice among others. Here are a few suggestions.

Can we hope that, taking into account the new situation of evangelization in this world, the Catholic Church would join with other denominations, for example at the Ecumenical Council of Churches in Geneva, to address the most urgent needs of this time and join in plans for action? Can we ask the Church to acknowledge that the new culture should not be seen as a risk but an opportunity to dialogue with all of humankind? Can the Church be partners in the Internet and in satellite communications, not only to express itself, but also to listen, dialogue, and stimulate according to the Spirit dwelling in us? Can we expect that our Church will descend more and more into the marketplace? John Paul II through his journeys makes a great move of the Church into the world. Can we imagine that he would dare to participate in public debates on television, questioned by great journalists?

By learning to be one voice among others, the Church has the hope of feeling lighter and more liberated. While the loss of some of its secular powers may make it less powerful in worldly terms, the Church has an opportunity to become "all things to all people" (1 Corinthians 9:22). As such it will become a more powerful influence on the human heart and consequently the world will better listen to what the Church has to say. Maybe then with other denominations it will be able to invent some new gestures. The theologian Raimundo Panikkar in "The Christian Challenge in the Third Millennium" dared to write: "My reflection leads us to plead not for an exclusively Christian Vatican III council . . . but for a 'concilium,' a call for the reconciliation of all the human race . . . a Jerusalem II after Jerusalem I where the question of circumcision was discussed. For new times, new audacity."[2]

——) The Culture of the Media Needs Paul's Language

From my viewpoint, the Gospel will not be integrated into the new culture if Paul is not granted the right to challenge language and attitudes. The bishop of Hull, in an interview on Radio-Canadian television, suddenly reversed roles, turned back to the interviewer, and asked him, "Who are the people most difficult to interview on TV?" The interviewer answered right away, "Politicians and Church people, because they will only say what they think that they are obliged to say and not what they think."

How can the Gospel be made present to a television audience without promoting two attitudes, two languages, one more institutional and the other more personal and ready to dialogue? It should be at the same time the words of the bishops and that of another voice with an image language even vague and disturbing. Who will be the last to exaggerate or rave remains to be seen, but we should remember the story of Apollos in the Acts of the Apostles, "He began to speak boldly in the synagogue, but when Priscilla and Aquila heard him, they took him aside, and explained the way of God to him more accurately" (Acts 18:26).

When Bishop Decourtray asked the Archbishop of Paris how he should speak on television, the Archbishop answered, "If you believe in God people will see it!" What matters above all is the testimony of a living faith in Christ. This is what the audience will see and remember. Accustomed today to public debates and interviews with heads of state, the public can perceive the difference between the person who speaks on behalf of the hierarchical and official Church and the faithful member of the Church who speaks on behalf of the Holy Spirit. The Gospel should fear a muzzled speech more than a free one, a uniform attitude more than a varied one.

What could be, and what is already, the language, the attitude of those who follow in the media the path of Paul?

- First of all, Paul says "I." He is going to expose his disputes, his journeys, his fears, and his visions. We should read the epistles to the Corinthians again. We will meet there a strong character of flesh and blood. Speaking on the media means daring to compromise one's self and risk being criticized for saying "I," not only "I think" but "I am what I think."

- Secondly, Paul uses words like "yes" or "no," clear and strong, muscled, well-defined gestures and images apt to strike the audience. You will succeed on television if you speak the truth like the Gospel, "If you think yes" (Matthew 7:27). The journalist Elkaback said to Cardinal Decourtray, "Don't be afraid! Tell me three issues on which you frankly disagree without any nuances and you will succeed very well on television." The cardinal declared without nuance against the death penalty. He received more than 700 letters in response!

- Thirdly, Paul's word is emotional, fed not only on doctrine but also on feeling. We should speak on behalf of a burning sensation more than a philosophy, on behalf of the secret giving sense to our life and not to please the audience. A Canadian once explained to us how every politician had to practice what he called "artistic skating," that is, speaking without saying anything. Contrary to that artificial language, we should remember the violent stand of the Abbé Pierre against some French and African politicians, his dramatic calls in the great winter cold in favor of the homeless! The education in seminaries and universities that ignored affective values in favor of the rational ones did not help to prepare a generation able to express today the Gospel on television.

- Finally, Paul's word brings together weakness and strength. Speaking with emotion means wearing weakness, not an iron mask. It means wearing a sense of vulnerability, not impermeability. It is not easy to accept weakness! Yet this is a radical point that distinguishes evangelization from all other forms of political communication. The politician must never appear weak. He is strong or he falls down. The evangelist on the contrary enjoys his weakness so that Christ's strength may shine forth. It is the paradox of evangelization linked to the most prestigious techniques! On television, it is not the power of rational arguments that will best convince a large audience, but the weakness containing a transcendental strength. When the missionary recognizes himself as inconsistent and unforeseeable, he is the strongest. Then in him the Creator and Savior is manifested. In order that the radical dependence of the being should show, some people leave their speeches unfinished, retaining points that they are unsure of. This way they hope that the Person dwelling in them will reveal himself through some spontaneous phrase. Faith comes from a deeper lever than that of reason. It comes from the vibration of one soul to another one. Being touched by grace is nothing less than experiencing such a vibration in the soul that cannot be explained.

The proof of God is letting weakness show so that the intimate Strength can be revealed.

——) Go to the Barbarians

Paul had heard in a dream the words, "Come over to Macedonia to help us" (Acts 16:9). He dared enter into the world of the barbarians, those who did not share the Jewish culture, the idle men of Greece and the dockyard workers of Corinth. The "barbarians" of today are countless, all the people who speak a different language than that spoken by the traditional Church. Obviously throughout the centuries, the Churches made up a particular language. It is a language established through the customs and rules of thousands of religious orders, not only a code of laws, but of a lifestyle, a wisdom strongly marked by the encyclicals, with catechisms as their secure form. Quite in contrast to this language there is the language of the media, creative, linked to events, personalized, with different meanings, like the image. Doubtless the traditional formulas of the Church must continue to be expressed and taught. Nevertheless it is necessary to shift to stereo, to a language with two channels. Not only the formal language, but also nonverbal language, the language of new formulas and of striking images, the language of voice and of politically committed actions.

Everything should not be expressed through channel "mono-1," dominated by the official language. The freedom of being and speaking differently should be left to the disciples of Paul. It is a complementary language spoken in the spirit of communion, spoken with a mutual respect and the will to "influence one another."

Reviving the productive tension of distance and communion between Peter and Paul is the condition for the evangelization of the new culture.

—) Reflections on Pluralism

When we are simply one pavilion in the huge international fair, we can think that we are the best one; we can think that we own the truth and have the secret of life. However, we cannot prevent others from thinking differently and believing they are the best. Thank God, we believe that Christ is "the Way, the Truth, and the Life" for all human beings. There is no problem in saying "as Christians, we believe that . . ." But in no case can such a belief be *imposed,* neither on behalf of economic power, nor on behalf of a culture, and still less on behalf of reason and knowledge. Faith can only be *offered*.

That was true yesterday. The encyclical on missionary activity is explicit. "The Church proposes, never imposes. She respects people and cultures just as she presents faith before the altar of conscience." This affirmation has become an imperative in our modern culture.

Speaking via the media means accepting pluralism. Obviously this was not always Paul's way, both because of the culture of this time and also because of his abrupt temper. At least we should follow Paul in his will to open himself entirely to all, a Jew with the Jews, outside the law to those outside the law. (See 1 Corinthians

9:19–23.) In many countries today, the question of pluralism replaces the old debate on secularity. Little by little, our Church becomes accustomed to secularity. Will she take the same step toward pluralism? "The central conflict in today's Church," writes the American sociologist and novelist Andrew Greeley, "is between those who favor pluralism and those who favor centralization."[3]

I will now speak of pluralistic dialogue. By that I mean the dialogue as such, which of course can take place between an inferior and a superior, even if the latter has the last word. I shall speak of the form of dialogue requiring equality of partnership in communication and freedom to form one's own conclusions. Such a dialogue, as open as it may be, has nothing to do with passive tolerance, or any sort of detachment from one's self and the world. It demands activity, compromise, knowledge of one's partners, of their history, of their psychology and their positions. It also demands some degree of perspective on one's own ideals and personal beliefs. The proverb is true. "What should they know of England who only England know?" Such a dialogue is also the opposite of blurred speech, in half tones, inspired by the fear of committing one's self. Christ accuses those who blush because of him. Christians know they are promoting an alternative society, a counterculture. They may wait for the favorable time to speak, but they cannot hide their treasure. We are in dialogue in the world of the media; we are not the children of the media.

It is a tricky attitude that is important to deepen. The foundation of our pluralism is not the necessity of a horizontal agreement between the members, though such a harmony would be precious. Basically our pluralism is rooted in the acknowledgment of transcendence, both of God and of our partners, a two-sided transcendence. This voice from beyond all tells me, you cannot conceal God's transcendence, that God who is God springing up from your chaos, from your ruins and from your joys. You must speak; you must express that Sun burning in you, that Gospel which fascinates you. You must speak of the necessity dwelling in you. You must also speak on behalf of that transcendence and freedom in others. Acknowledging transcendence forbids any deadly action or psychological manipulation. It forbids you to judge as well as to shoot. Are you greater than God to have the right to kill anyone who does not think like you? Are you more in a hurry to condemn than God who waits for the time of the harvest to separate truth from falseness?

Our attitude of pluralistic dialogue finds its justification in the transcendence of God and of his ways. Haven't we forgotten this too often? But what is interesting for us here is pointing to this particular aspect: the media culture imperatively requires evangelization, not only in respect but also in accepting equality with their dialogue partners and their freedom, in positive sympathy for whatever paths they may take.

—) Dialogue and Inculturation

After defining inculturation as "a theological term of the cultural model of the incarnation," the Indian theologian Michael Amaladoss writes, "Unfortunately the Christian discourse on inculturation calls up the image of the Gospel going out in the world to conquer cultures, to express itself in them, integrate them and so enrich them. We almost never hear that the Gospel itself has cultural limitations and could have something to learn . . . the sole option for us is not incarnation but dialogue that prepares us to receive as well as to give. This means that incarnation might not be the paradigm to be utilized in order to understand the process of the encounter between Gospel and culture. I believe that the process of the encounter between Gospel and culture is not incarnation but dialogue." Later on, Amaladoss will distinguish the great religions from the popular religious traditions and after observing that mission has been successful only when it has met the popular traditions not yet enslaved by a great religion, he thinks that with the great religions "the mission can only take the form of dialogue lived in mutual respect."[4]

We share Amaladoss's viewpoint about the necessity and the form of pluralistic dialogue. The arguments are different. For Amaladoss it is the incarnation of the great religions in particular cultures that makes dialogue imperative. We believe that it is the nature of the electronic culture that makes it so. In creating an indefinite multiplicity of communications and opening up the marketplace, technology leads to pluralistic communication. If we think of the big computers performing at the rate of 150 billion operations a second, we perceive an attempt to distinguish and connect everything. How can those with such technology at their disposal imagine the future of humankind outside of unity in diversity? How can they fail to experiment with the incredible development in the possibility of choice? In view of such a future, the pluralistic dialogue is offered as the only coherent voice, faithful to the signs of the times. To refuse pluralism would mean to turn our back on the technologies that underpin modern culture.

The Christian notices that the argument of authority that aims at proclaiming a compulsory truth for everyone is no longer acceptable in this culture. Moreover by discovering the deepest meaning of the culture, the Christian can reach a better understanding of the very being of God, pluralistic in his transcendence and his trinity. This pluralism is highlighted by cultural techniques and movements that lead the Christian to a better apprehension of hidden and dormant truths. Pluralism is not a demonic but a divine attitude. It is the condition of the unity of the world and of a new evangelization.

At the height of the pluralistic dialogue, Amaladoss speaks of unity in terms of harmony and his best example is taken from music. In the same way, in the audiovisual world, I suggest that the summit can be found in the art of mixing, which has nothing to do with guiding the mixture under the power of "his excellency the word." A good mix supposes as a base knowledge and respect of the sources—sound, word, image—to obtain a marriage producing a unified language that is harmonious and humanly significant. Knowledge and respect of each source are necessary from the start. The marriage (the mix) is the end. The future is not inculturation but marriage.

Through managing a multicultural formation program in religious communications, I came to develop some ways of acting and speaking more precisely. We could call them "the ten commandments of pluralistic dialogue"! Of course these are not laws, but attitudes that make the spirit more concrete and relevant to various situations.

1. A clear distinction must be established between what I sincerely believe as a person and what the Church professes. It may happen that for reasons of character, evolution, or political necessity I would not be able to fully agree on this or that point. But, by my union with the Church as a baptized believer, I respect what the Church

teaches. To say, "I think that . . ." is different from saying, "As Catholics we believe that. . . ." At the end of his life Graham Greene speaking of his faith recognized humbly, "I have faith, I pray God that he would give me the belief."[5]

2. To be respectful and tolerant of all beliefs and practices, except on this point: the killing of human life, and the essential freedom that belongs to it.

3. To try to discern positively the ways the spirit is working in various religions and societies. The latter can bring us inspiration and help. "Hearing" in the evangelical sense is the first step in discernment.

4. To present faith as an invitation. I invite you, I do not force you to come or follow me. I do not say, "It is the only way." I only say, "It is the way I experience and believe to be the best one."

5. To try to build up universal communion, especially by a concrete commitment to meet the great issues of our time, with special attention given to the outcasts of the world.

6. Proposing the faith also requires strong words. It is good that impulses of indignation, even anger should spring up in us, as in the language Jesus used when he expelled the moneylenders from the temple. Other circumstances demand clear statements and persuasion. Sometimes we have to use words that cut us off from the foundation. It is necessary that they take place in a spirit of dialogue and do not destroy in a serious way the path to communion between persons and organizations.

7. To refuse to rehash old debates with young people. To be free and respectful in matters of dress, rites, words, of gender representation, etc.

8. To acknowledge that the Roman Catholic group is not the only one that makes present Christ and the Gospel. Ecumenism is a permanent context for our words and actions. The ecumenical practice should utilize common activities rather than doctrinal discussions to meet the great troubles of the world.

9. To recognize the different religious, doctrinal, and pastoral sensitivities in the Church as complementary, always partial approaches to the God who knows. It does not mean that everything should be blessed, but that the Spirit must be discerned in the differences of the concrete ways leading us to truth and harmony.

10. To begin with the sharing of goods. Sharing ideas and doctrines must come second; to be pluralistic in a culture of the media means work: personal contact, mutual service, and sharing of meals and celebrations.

According to my experience acquired in more than twenty years of working with African, American, Latin, and Anglo-Saxon cultures, I can say that most of the so-called doctrinal misunderstandings came from our being unconsciously locked into a rhythm and sensitivity of a particular culture. The pluralistic dialogue requires a reasonable knowledge of Catholic doctrine and faithful attention to the Holy Spirit. Yet a really pluralistic person is the one who acknowledges the mystery of his or her own life. Those who experience the solitude of their consciousness, the fickleness of their emotions, and the ignorance of their own destiny are better able to let others have their own right-of-way, detours, and expressions. Approaching the message in terms of the body rather than doctrine, they could not rashly criticize a concrete body and the history it contains. Ultimately, in Christian terms, should not "compassion" be present when we are in the midst of disagreements?

⎯) **T**he Shaken-Up Church, a Providential Opportunity

Derrick de Kerckhove, author of *The Skin of Culture* showed how electronics in a way extends the human skin to the universe. In his latest book, *Connected Intelligence: The Arrival of the Web Society,* de Kerckhove argues that the planet has displaced the human being as the norm of everything.[6] We live in a world of interactivity, worldwide applications, virtual reality, and hypertext. This means to me that the Church is now undergoing a major shock at the dawn of the new millennium.

This is not a deadly shock, but a vital one. The Church must now become a missionary once again, but missionary in a different way.

Why be a Christian if not for mission? In this age of the wonderful blossoming of intelligence, the expansion of the human species around the world, it is a scandal that the Church remains too exclusively a community of salvation for its members, rather than for the universe. In the Old Testament, Israel was elected to be a leaven to the world, the forerunner of a new civilization. This should also be the role of the Church in the modern world. Instead, the Church has become much too conservative, more concerned with the banking of faith in an attempt to preserve a subculture. It is more concerned with guarding doctrinal faithfulness for the flock than speaking toward leading a "total life" in and for the world.

The philosopher Paul Ricoeur describes the conditions under which the world's churches must enter the twenty-first century. "First of all I believe that the great confessions have to pay a huge price to survive. First, renounce all kinds of power that are not the power of a weak word. Second, compassion should take the place of doctrine. Ultimately each church should understand that it is place of commitment, but it is not the sole repository of truth. . . . Consequently it is not syncretism, skimming surface beliefs, that enhances the communication among churches. Rather each church should deepen itself and somehow shorten the distance to the other in depth."[7]

Ricoeur outlines in a few radical sentences the ways for the Church of tomorrow to resume and rejuvenate its mission. More than ever, when borders are disintegrating, we have to reconsider the substructure of the Church of Christ. The goal of this substructure is not the "re-establishment" of the group but the spreading of the salt. It is necessary today to invent a new "image" for the presence of the Risen Christ in the world. This is not an image of stones or catechisms, but a structure similar to that of an airport. It is a structure that is primarily oriented toward intercommunication and stimulation of the world. Christians connected to the Source they call Father have a wonderful power to make a more "energetic" sound for the world.

If it were not for the Spirit, Christians would not be able to be steady; to surmount the impossible, to transfigure what cannot be changed, to face persecution, old age, and death. The technoworld is longing for a freer, more spiritual, more universal life. We have to reactivate Paul, Paul beyond the walls to meet this longing. We have to find a new balance for pastoral activity, to create a substructure of spiritual revitalization of humankind, a substructure of multimedia dialogue, a missionary substructure of appeal and stimulation.

Then it will be said, let's hear it for technology, and let's hear it for the media, pushing the Church outside of its old walls!

—) Questions for Reflection

1. How has the perception of the Church's status in society changed in the modern world?

2. What principles from Paul the Apostle can help you become a more effective evangelizer?

3. What are the Ten Commandments of pluralistic dialogue? How can these be implemented?

4. How can you respond to the opportunities for mission that the new media environment gives to you?

CHAPTER 7

And in the Parishes?

Parishes are a necessity; "in Spirit and in truth,"
they have a great future.

We did not originally intend to speak of parish life in this book. But
when people read the manuscript they would ask, "What happens
with parishes with this kind of pastoral approach?" Today, parish
structures are the object of many debates, especially in countries like
French Canada where, during the last thirty years, religious obser-
vance dropped from 80 percent to 4 percent. Must we stay with the
classical parish structure or develop electronic parish structures? In
Toronto, McLuhan's school developed the idea that parishes seemed
to be entities created with one function in mind, a place where people were able to go to Church.

I am speaking as a person who does not have wide experience
in parish ministry. I ask questions in an electronic key. When electronic communications transform people into angelic beings, when
automobiles, airplanes, mobile telephones, and the Internet meta-
morphose my rural body, what happens to the village church? I open
my eyes. Is the Church becoming a neighborhood store, while malls
are now being superimposed on my life, placing a claim on my finan-
cial interests and many of my choices? On one hand it is in the parish
church where we find older people attached to their neighborhood.
On the other we find the vast crowds at Lourdes and Taizé. Brother
Roger, founder and prior of Taizé, seeing this evolution once told me,

"*I* worry . . . because young people do not go to the local Mass, do not go to church any more." And I answered him, "But they are coming to Taizé."

It would be a wrong strategy to pit neighborhood schools and churches against the electronic local and worldwide communication. The electronic world does not oppose or destroy; it modifies and makes possible many surprising mixtures. Human beings always will need Mother Earth and home. People cannot leave those places without being lost. The parish church is the Mother Earth and one of the fundamental places where people find a coherent sense of life. But just as radio and television were added to writing, the new media, electronic relationships and assemblies should little by little add to the geographical parish. It is not the local parish that is disappearing, but *a kind* of local parish. The hour has come to integrate the media into the Church's way of life. Toward which future are we headed?

In the beginning was the rural parish, tied to the land. It was the time when we were going to church on horseback or on foot. At that time speech and the theater prevailed. Then the book came along and slowly the parish became a seminary. In those days, the catechism, the missal, schools, mission, and social service reigned supreme. Parishes were judged to be successful or not on the basis of statistical surveys.

Then the petty electronic god made its appearance, not all that bad, but impudent and noisy. The old stone churches slowly emptied out. A lot of people, most of them young, went elsewhere, or nowhere, armed with a remote control. Many went to see the exciting concerts with their electronic modulation. Among the most aware it became a habit to consult their inner compass to know where or with whom to go. The Master has said, "Time will come when I will no longer be adored in this place or in that, but in spirit and in truth." And that seems the future of the parish, "spiritualization" from an interior wide-awake state.

We cannot reduce parish evolution to the petty god of electronic impulses. But I still consider that individuals are the main power of this evolution of the parish and that God's grace works through this petty god. We can see the changing direction better when we look at the patterns in the media. I distinguish three directions. These directions are not dreams without reality, but realizations or beginnings that are important to underline the meaning.

The three are: (1) the developing potential of new communication technologies (the media technology aspect), (2) the development of relational communities (the media network aspect), and (3) the preponderance of spiritual communities (the development of the personal choices inherent in the media).

——) Making Use of Communication Technologies

A Methodist minister at Drew University near New York City has experimented with a new type of sermon using a computer within worship. The organization is complex. It requires electronic facilities that are not accessible everywhere. But such experiences indicate the direction. We are headed toward interactive communication, combining visuals and sound. After the Council of Trent, the sermon was supposed to teach and explain the catechism. This a parish priest like the Curé of Ars did with resounding success. Following the advent of electronic communication technologies, the sermon, without abandoning instruction, became a dialogue with the Word of God.

Let's underline some aspects. In the time of generalization of feedback (audience surveys, bar coding) we would not hold on in the traditional mode. Priests and preachers represent the unity of doctrine, but they are presently restricted to a monologue style of preaching. The introduction of *dialogue communication* in devotions and parish life is essential and it already appears in many ways. In the collective preparation of rituals, in the responses of the laity, in families taking charge of the sacraments (baptism, marriage, funerals, anointing of the sick, etc.) there is partnership in religious education, bulletins, and parish radio (for instance Radio-City in Geneva). What we need for the future parish is not the elimination of responsible priests and experts, but a parish based on the interests of 80 percent of the people and with a realistic pastoral plan (financing, human fulfillment, recruiting). Such developments will not be done in the name of the theory of parishes, but according to the exigencies of communication.

The techniques? Some parish churches are equipped with large screens and spectacular panels. This was not done without reactions from authorities or certain parishioners. Will we see computer systems allowing instant dialogue between parishioners or with the preachers and priests? Why not? Responsible parish leaders in the field are the only ones who can judge as "good shepherds." This supposes that they know the technologies, their chance of succeeding, and the risks to the faith. This also requires a formation that can teach people how to find the way through our feelings to open up to the spiritual. There is the predominance of the ear over the image, the value of a suggestive and imperfect image rather than a warm and illustrative one, space and reverberation.[1] We will always have to choose between a popular path, more spectacular and attractive, but more superficial, and a more targeted way, less formal but more intimate and suggestive.

—) Developing Relational Communities

What should a young priest do upon entering a new parish? It is the same for the parish as in opening a Christian radio station. He will begin with neither the technology, nor even the money, nor a professional approach. He will begin by creating a network of friends, a network of devoted followers. If he has the fire in his heart, if he is passionately and energetically involved, groups will gather around him, and then the enterprise, the money, and the professionalism will come. There are so many today searching for the meaning of their life and waiting for the vibration of an appeal.

The starting point of parish vitality is the relational community. At this level, priests and parish leaders must first focus on mutual identification, support, and forgiveness, networks of family and friends. "See how they love one another." If there is a time when this citation from the early church takes on its full meaning, it is right now, in this age of the media.

I mean by a relational community (some would call it a networking community) a group of persons linked by common interests, especially by human relationships, that is, by common feelings of age, tastes, and vision of the world. These persons need one another; they are willing to converse and to meet in order to pray, to realize projects together, and to dialogue. We can ask all people attending Mass to give to one another the kiss of peace, but we cannot ask them to need or wish to talk to one another. We need a fundamental step, one that provides for people's primary needs. There is the need to be in dialogue with one's neighbors, the need to share worries, the need to be known, the need of help and warmth, the need to meet stimulating personalities and masters of wisdom. It is their recognition of these personal needs that enables some groups to inject new blood into the larger parish.

Parishes will have to fulfill the needs and the communication dynamic generated by the media in any way they can. The media understand how to address these needs. The audiences are asking for an announcer who will fulfill their solitude, a singer who will make them dream of a paradise, a star who will appeal to their greater aspirations, a voice that will touch them to the bottom of their hearts.

The media responded to that expectation with the Beatles, Michael Jackson, and the Spice Girls. These are superstars who have conquered crowds and generated, with system support, electronic networks of T-shirt-dressed fans, repeating the symbolic gesture of their stars. Is the starting point communication models, the media style, television and radio? Religious programs must act according to these rules. A nonpracticing old woman on her deathbed calls a priest who asks, "Why are you asking me to come over, when I never saw you in church?" The woman answers, "I promised the TV priest I would do it." There has been an intimate communication between this woman and the priest celebrating the Sunday TV Mass. This is the kind of personal, intimate, warm communication we have to develop in parishes, having recourse to networks of friends and of phone, fax, and Internet surfers. I believe that parishes will be vigorous if they are supported and nourished by relational communities, which, before being highly religious, live deeply among themselves a fraternity of the heart, that in fact originates from Christ.

——) Developing Spiritual Communities

We cannot be satisfied only with interest and relational groups, however essential they are for parishes. The target is the spiritual community, either through the presence of profoundly spiritual personalities in the middle of the relational groups or by the resource groups whose direct aim is spiritual development—in monasteries, spiritual families, organizations for retired people, and the like.

Here are the specifics for the spiritual community. It directly gathers the people in their reason for being and living. Here we don't meet to achieve external goals, but first to reveal and to stimulate ourselves to live fully. It could be convenient to meet for evangelization or for purposes of spiritual formation. We could also meet to accomplish some good work. But the initial purpose for our meeting is to allow each member of the group to become established in his or her vocation and to accomplish what they really want to do. In the process, we accept each person's awkwardness.

The chief characteristic of a Christian community is that it shares the Gospel. But this community is more than one that simply shares some acknowledgment of Christ or the moral applications from the Beatitudes. It is about sharing Christ as the source and the subject of my life. It is what I am in Christ that stimulates others; it is not simply what I repeat from books. Speaking in the language of the media, a Christian community is the vibration of Christ in ourselves. Is this not the sense in which we must understand the Gospel words, "When two or three gather in my name, I will be with them"? A Christian community exists when, evoking Jesus memory, our heart hums because he reveals to us, through others, the meaning of our life. This "gift of Christ" can surely be communicated when we share words, but also when we are keeping silent, creating an atmosphere, giving a silent glance, demonstrating attitudes that are unusual during a formal sharing of the Gospel. I dare to say that the essential thing that is going on here is "the common vibration of hearts." This is not an "affective soup," but the emotion that gives the mutual recognition of the Master in our lives. This is the "Ah, Lord God!" that Jeremiah utters when God calls him (Jeremiah 1:6).

How is such a spiritual community linked to the culture of the media, a culture that is rather extroverted and mundane? The electronic technologies above all invite human beings to make constant personal choices. Without these choices the people are at risk of being drowned in the wave of information and emotions. To be detached from material things appeals to those who are growing in the spirit. The dilemma in the new culture is simple: either I lose my soul and am at the mercy of the wind, or I live in the spirit. It is fascinating to become a "super angel" when the walls of the old formula are cracking. But it is a shame to see the possibility of surfing anywhere on the Net, if we cannot reckon with an awakened inner being. The spiritual community represents not only a way to survive in this world, but also the best way to be awake to the Spirit in one's self. It is when it starts from that wide-awake state and from a spiritual stimulation that life can be fulfilled strongly and actively in the media culture.

The existence of such spiritual communities, as the presence of spiritual "articulators" in the middle of the groups, should constitute the ultimate target of the parish pastoral approach. Tomorrow we will not find ourselves externally constrained to say, "Go to Mass," but we will do so out of interior necessity. Without doubt this is when we are called to mix the most innovative actions in our pastoral ministry.

Here are a few points as examples. Religious education has held that its main object is to teach the catechism. Should it not rather have as its main goal the spiritual awakening of the participant? From childhood, we have been trained to keep silent and to listen to interior voices and spiritual sharing between brothers and sisters. We must think about the local liturgy. It must be more than making the Mass and sermon interesting. We must also create an appropriate surrounding of light and sound, awakening a taste for interior silence and the habit of personal meditation on God's word: the very center of the liturgical act.

What is most important is the awakening of what we can call "the interior necessity." We need not believe that such an orientation will abolish catechism, baptisms, funerals, and works of charity. It is not a question of abolishing but of rethinking our priorities and directing our efforts to those that call forth spirituality, awakening and accompanying of persons, and the sharing of spiritual goods.

Finally, what should we evoke in our formation in seminaries and pastoral institutions? Without abandoning a serious intellectual apprenticeship of theology, it is important to mix more profoundly the theological formation with a spiritual, sensory, and technical formation. It is also important to introduce into the languages of this world a mission perspective of globalization.

Parishes are a necessity; "in Spirit and in truth," they have a great future.

—) **Questions for Reflection**

1. How should parishes respond to the new media environment?

2. What is the importance of creating "relational" communities in the parish? What can you contribute to creating such a community in your parish?

3. How can parishes support the spiritual needs of their members? What are some of the first steps you can take to bring this about in your parish?

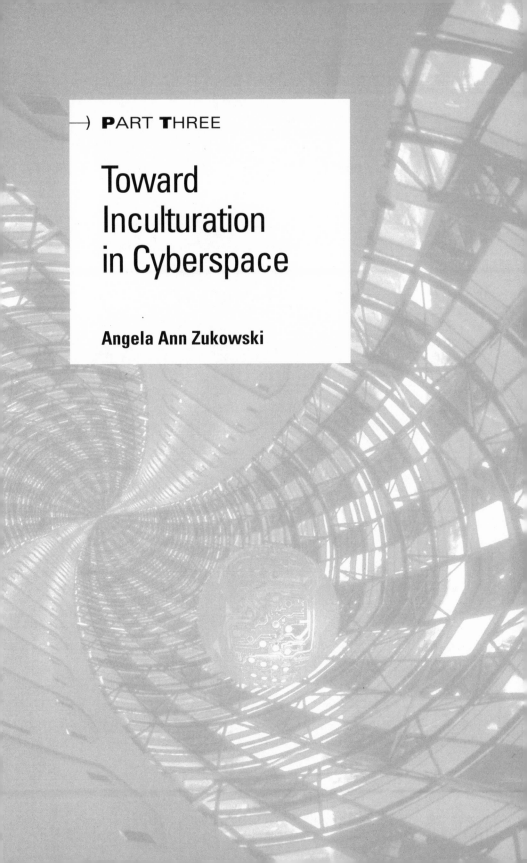

PART THREE

Toward Inculturation in Cyberspace

Angela Ann Zukowski

Evangelization in the New Mediasphere

Our young people are voting with their feet and moving out of parish and church life as they discover that the delivery of the message is becoming irrelevant and not meaningful in their lives. Note—we are not saying the "message" but the "delivery of the message." Delivery means a lot; it is how the message is packaged!

—⟩ The Challenge of the New Evangelization

The religious landscape described in an earlier chapter demonstrates the complex challenge the evangelizer faces in the coming years. We stand amidst a cacophony of voices that may confuse us. For there are those who would tell us it is the "worst of times" while others proclaim it is "the best of times" for venturing forth with the Good News into the rapidly unfolding new landscape. However, those who believe realize that "we are supposed to let the word of grace come to us and to let the word of the Gospel be grasped not just by our ears and our minds, but also at that place within ourselves where we stand before God with our freedom and love."[1]

We realize that evangelization today is not merely proselytizing or a form of cultural imperialism, as it may have been projected or perceived in the past. A new era has dawned! Perhaps the new religious panorama in which we live reminds us that we truly are an Advent people. We realize that while God's offer already has been revealed in the world it is yet to be fully received, understood, and accepted. It is necessary for the evangelizer to find innovative ways to break open the Good News through word, image, story, and song that stimulate the religious imagination of the hearers to desire to respond—to say "Amen."

This chapter attempts to further advance our conversation on the highlights of evangelization with particular attention to the diverse cultural understandings of the what and how of evangelization. We conclude by seeking out a possible relationship between marketing and evangelization.

New conversations triggered by the overture of a new evangelization have enabled us to begin to perceive various preliminary approaches that orchestrate the way for effective evangelization. This fourfold preliminary approach is represented by (1) our way of being (or presence), (2) the environment, (3) authentic listening, and (4) action within our cultural contexts. A personal story may illustrate my point.

In the 1960s my first mission found me ministering among the indigenous North American peoples in Colorado. One day I was sent on a mission to engage in a visitation and Catholic census on a nearby Navajo reservation. I impressively remember to this day the Navajo woman who represents for me the significance of the fourfold approach for effective evangelization.

I found my Navajo woman weaving outside her home, which is called a hogan. I approached her and began a battery of predetermined questions expecting some traditional answers or responses. She simply looked at me and smiled while continuing to work her loom. The initial lack of verbal communication on her part made me feel uncomfortable. Soon I found myself extending my farewell and departing. I left concerned and perplexed. What had happened? It appeared that nothing had happened.

I returned to Cortez and immediately visited one of our Native American parishioners. I communicated my experience and my frustration of not being able to communicate with or trigger a response from the Navajo woman. My friend smiled and gently laughed. She said: "You perceived that nothing happened because it didn't match your predetermined expectations or desired outcomes of the visit. What did you expect?" My friend proceeded to encourage me to reconsider my initial approach. What other alternatives for engaging the Navajo woman were possible? I began making a neat list of techniques to realize my missionary goal. My friend laughed again, saying: "You still have it wrong." She advised me to return the next day to the Navajo weaver woman. "Approach her with reverence," she said. "Assume a place next to the weaver woman and her loom and sit silently with her. Thus," she said, "you will begin to realize your mission."

Well, for the next few weeks I would occasionally stop by the hogan and quietly sit beside the weaver woman who appeared undisturbed and quite welcoming to my presence beside her (presence). As time went by, I became more comfortable with the silence. I began to see and hear elements of nature around me that had escaped me before in my eagerness to speak (listening). In the silence of our presence to one another I became attuned to the artistic expression and rhythm of her weaving. I began to realize the significance and the impact of the environment for our presence to one another (environment). The consistent shuffling of the shuttle between and across the threads was a mantra of sorts. It calmed my inner being. I soon found that I looked forward to simply being present with the weaver in silence. In the silence I was thrust into a profound world of spiritual encounter with the world and this woman in a way I could not have imagined.

One morning as I approached the woman by her loom and became comfortable in my now familiar sacred space she turned to me and said: "You know, Sister, several weeks ago our spirits joined. In our silent presence with one another we were woven into deep communion. Have you felt it? What has it said to you? You first came to me with so many words. Your vision was narrow. In the silence I have learned much about you and I hope you about my people our land and myself. Now are there questions or comments you wish to make to me (action)?" Well, what could I say? So many of my initial questions appeared no longer to be relevant to the context. I the evangelizer was being evangelized! As we proceeded to tell stories about our spiritual experiences of the All Holy, I found we had much in common as women and seekers of spiritual truth. Our stories bound us together and opened new doors of spiritual awareness and enlightenment. As I unveiled the encounters of the first Christian community with the person of Jesus, she saw parallels and connections with her own experiences. Thus, it was through presence, listening, and environment that the Good News was proclaimed.

You too may find similar stories in your lives that break open the Word.

Scripture is filled with stories that communicate similar encounters of individuals with God that radically changed their lives. Consider for a moment the prophet Ezekiel. He has a religious experience. He is in touch with God. He is inspired to write down his religious experience, but the experience is not to remain in written "material" form. God says to Ezekiel "eat what is offered to you; eat this scroll, and go, speak to the house of Israel" (Ezekiel 3:1). So Ezekiel opens his mouth and eats the scroll. The same key elements of presence, environment, listening, and action are what is needed to proclaim the Word. Remember it is not just the eating of the scroll but the going out to speak and to witness what one has received that completes the revelation and the story. The message, as with Ezekiel, must become bone of our bone and flesh of our flesh. Thus, we learn from this story that evangelizing primarily radiates from our very presence, from being receptive and active in the world.

The invitation to be a messenger of God has not always been received with a lot of enthusiasm and understanding. There are many who were reluctant prophets, fearful of the context and the people they were being called upon to speak with. Consider Moses, Jonah, Amos, Elijah, and others. Let's reflect for a moment upon Elijah. Here he is on top of a mountain hiding in a cave. Soon he is called out of the cave and commanded to wait for the Lord "to pass by." He waits in fear and trembling. How will the Lord come? What will the Lord request? With what force, power, and awesomeness will the Lord appear? Several encounters unnerve Elijah. He experiences a strong powerful wind that crushes the rocks around him, an earthquake, and a fire. Yet, the Lord was in none of these unusual experiences. 1 Kings 19:12 indicates that the Lord comes in "a sound of sheer silence." It was so ordinary. "A sound of sheer silence." In this encounter with the profound "Mystery of Life" the Lord called forth from Elijah presence, listening, and action. For the Lord commanded Elijah not to stay hidden with his fears or to remain at the entrance to the cave meditating on the awesome mysterious encounter but go forth to invoke, anoint, and break open the Word to the Israelite people. This was no small task that the Lord called Elijah to complete.

So today it is no small task that we who are baptized are called to accomplish in the contemporary world! Our baptismal covenant commissions us to unveil and reveal the "Gracious Mystery" of God-with-us. Bacik indicates that for many people today this Gracious Mystery is hidden, forgotten, distorted, or encased in a zone of silence.[2] Thus, like Elijah and Ezekiel our evangelizing mission is to reveal the Gracious Mystery and break open the Word.

——) The Invitation of *Evangelii Nuntiandi*

Let us reflect on those three questions posed in *Evangelii Nuntiandi.*

In our day, what has happened to that hidden energy of the Good News, which is able to have a powerful effect on man's conscience?

To what extent and in what way is that evangelical force capable of really transforming the people of this century?

What methods should be followed in order that the power of the Gospel may have its effect? (#4)

These three questions pose a renewed challenge to engage in a paradigmatic shift in the way we evangelize in the new millennium. We find certain powerful, proactive, and energetic words articulate here. Consider the terms hidden energy, powerful effect, transforming, method*s*, power of the Gospel; what do they communicate to us? These terms are anything but passive or stagnant! They require the evangelist to seek out new methodologies (note the plural) in order to reveal and transform humanity in light of the Good News. The word *energy* here predicts excitement and change. It is a powerful word. *Webster's II New Riverside University Dictionary* defines as (1) vitality in expression, (2) the capacity for action or accomplishment. The word *energize* means (1) to impart energy to, or (2) to release or put out energy.[3]

What can our evangelizing efforts look and be like if we focus on the "energy" dimension of our ministry? Energy is infused everywhere. It reminds us that we are engaged in constant change. There is a process continually going on in and around us that is making life different whether or not we wish to acknowledge it consciously. If we look at energy from a theological context, is this not how we frequently refer to as the Holy Spirit? When Cardinal Suenens calls for a New Pentecost and Pope John Paul II calls for a New Evangelization effort, they are inviting us to get enthused about a spiritual movement that is living, dynamic, active, and shifting all the time. Evangelization is not about a singular activity or program but a way of *being*. *Being* is an active, not a passive, mode. It is a dynamic presence ever alert, attentive, and active in breaking open the Word in diverse and creative ways. For this reason the *General Directory for Catechesis* in referring to *Evangelii Nuntiandi* speaks of evangelization as a complex, rich, and dynamic reality (17) that must develop its "totality" (28) and completely incorporate its intrinsic bipolarity: witness and proclamation, (22) word and sacrament, (47) interior change and social transformation (18).[4]

—) Insights from the *General Directory for Chatechesis*

The *General Directory for Catechesis* (GDC) focuses on evangelization as the key principle of our catechetical efforts within the Church. Catechesis is understood as a moment in the process of evangelization. "These moments," the GDC states, "are not unique: they may be repeated, if necessary, as they give evangelical nourishment in proportion to the spiritual growth of each person or of the entire community" (49). It calls us to recognize that there is a new religious panorama "in which it is possible to distinguish three basic situations requiring particular and precise responses" (58). These are elaborated in the encyclical *Redemptoris Missio*. First, there is the situation of those "peoples, groups and sociocultural contexts in which Christ and his Gospel are not known, or which lack Christian communities sufficiently mature to be able to incarnate the faith in their own environment and proclaim it to other groups" (33). Its particular characteristic consists in the fact that it is directed to non-Christians and invites them to conversion. Second, "there are Christian communities with adequate and solid ecclesial structures. They are fervent in their faith and in Christian living." Here the directory calls for effective "pastoral action of the Church" to address their needs. And, third, in some younger Churches there exists "an intermediate situation," where "entire groups of the baptized have lost a living sense of the faith, or even no longer consider themselves members of the Church and live a life far removed from Christ and his Gospel" (33).

The *General Catechetical Directory* elaborates on the fact that each situation is different and each calls for a different response. Many of our local churches have the entire religious panorama to address. *Redemptoris Missio* says, "The boundaries between pastoral care of the faithful, new evangelization and specific missionary activity are not clearly definable, and it is unthinkable to create barriers between them or to put them into water-tight compartments" (34).

The GDC indicates that the methodological processes for effective catechesis (evangelization) is a dynamic process, consisting of

> various interactive elements: a listening in the culture of the people, to discern an echo (omen, invocation, sign) of the word of God; a discernment of what has an authentic Gospel value or is at least open to the Gospel; a purification of what bears the mark of sin (passions, structures of evil) or of human frailty; an impact on people through stimulating an attitude of radical conversion to God, of dialogue, and of patient interior maturation. (204)

The idea of a "patient interior maturation" is key. Rather than attempting to manipulate the culture there is a nurturing process that takes time. We are also aware that evangelization activities are not a single moment in the local church's life but an ongoing process. This process involves a dynamic that is ever alert, open, and respective for the people with whom the Good News is being proclaimed and lived.

The inculturation of the Good News is one of maturation, which requires authentic ongoing persistence in a dialogue of faith within the culture. This perspective makes it clear that evangelization must involve more than "getting people back to church" or even converting the unbaptized. In *Evangelii Nuntiandi,* Paul VI had a broader view of evangelization.

> For the church, evangelizing means bringing the Good News into all the strata of humanity and through its influence transforming humanity from within and making it new. (18)

In speaking about the transformation of humanity and making creation new, Pope Paul envisioned the work of evangelization in its wider scope. The kind of renewal spoken of involves "interior renewal which the Gospel calls *metanoia;* it is a radical conversion, a profound change of mind and heart" (#10).

The scriptures unfold a kaleidoscope of *metanoia* (conversion) experiences that formed the People of God. In the Old Testament we read about Abraham, Moses, Jacob, the Widow of Zaraphath, Samuel, Miriam, and the prophets who were summoned by an insistent God in such a way that the experience could only be called a right about-face, direct turnaround, or redirection to a calling. The basic elements of conversional change seem to be repeated in almost every Old Testament conversion experience, according to Gillespie. First, there is a flashing vision of truth. Then some kind of conviction of one's worthlessness. Next, the joy of being forgiven with the purging of absolution. And finally, one receives some kind of consciousness of new vision, personal mission, or life of service. This "sudden" model is multiplied throughout Old Testament Scripture.[5]

The New Testament records instances of change from one way of life to another. The disciples were called to follow Jesus; those who met Jesus of Nazareth were healed in spirit and called to follow a new way of life. In the Gospels we find the call of the disciples, Zacchaeus, Nicodemus, Mary Magdalene, the man born blind, Martha and Mary, the paralytic, the blind beggar, and others. In the Acts we read about the three thousand at Pentecost, the Greeks at Antioch, the Ethiopian eunuch, the jailer, Lydia, Paul, Barnabas—all were called to follow and were changed.[6]

Walter Conn builds on Lonergan's views on conversion in his seminal volume, *Christian Conversion: A Developmental Interpretation of Autonomy and Surrender,* and uses the same categories to understand conversional change. His discussion of the religious dimension of conversion is especially helpful as we come to understand Christian conversion as essentially an "invitation to a life not only dedicated to the love of neighbor but focused and empowered by the mysterious presence of God at its vital center."[7] This is an important dimension here. We are not merely talking about methods of organizing parishioners for the work of evangelization, but more essentially about ways of being open to God's grace that is at work in changing hearts. The Synod of Bishops for Oceania states clearly:

> [Conversion] is a call away from being exclusively inward looking and preoccupied with [the Church's] own needs, towards becoming outward looking and responding to the needs of others. It is in fact a radical call to holiness, to an ongoing change of heart, to a more evangelical lifestyle and to the realization of greater justice and love within the Christian community itself. It is a call to reconciliation, to renewal and reform of life in Jesus Christ and to greater fidelity to His Spirit.[8]

There are peak experiences and special moments, sometimes very dramatic moments, of radical conversion.

Nevertheless, conversion is not a once-and-for-all event. It is, rather, a lifelong process of hearing the Gospel more clearly and responding to it more fully. It is a profession of deepening faith and spiritual growth. It is a process that is reflected in living a lifestyle based more and more on the values of the reign of God. In light of this reality it is understandable that the *General Catechetical Directory* in speaking of the new religious panorama calls for a "comprehensive pastoral activity" (#59). In a pastoral letter to the diocese of Columbus, Ohio, Bishop James Griffin elaborates, "Very often today, local Churches are obliged to address the entire panorama. Conversion involves a constant journeying forward. As this journey calls us forward, it calls us to leave many things behind."[9]

Hearing the Good News and allowing it to transform our lives also sends us forward to proclaim the Good News to others. "You received without payment, give without payment" (Matthew 10:8). The cycle goes on not only in our own life of ever deepening faith, but also in our ever growing desire to share this faith with others. The Emmaus story (Luke 24:13–33) provides a beautiful example of this cycle. Notice that Jesus meets the disciples on the journey. He wants to know what they are talking about, to hear their story. He helps them understand their experience by imaging their story with the story of Scripture. They invite him to stay with them and recognize him in the breaking of the bread. Having experienced Jesus' presence in both word and sacrament, they go immediately to share this good news with their friends.

In *Go and Make Disciples: A National Plan and Strategy for Catholic Evangelization in the United States* the bishops of the United States explained how we evangelize

> by the way we live God's love in our daily life, by the love, example and support people give each other and by the ways parents pass faith on to their children; in our life as church, through the proclamation of the word and the wholehearted celebration of the saving deeds of Jesus; in renewal efforts of local and national scope; in the care we show to those most in need; in the ways we go about our work, share with our neighbors and treat the stranger. In daily life, family members evangelize each other, men and women their future spouses, and workers their fellow employees by the simple lives of faith they lead. Through the ordinary patterns of our Catholic life, the Holy Spirit brings about conversion and a new life in Christ.[10]

Jesus, at work in our lives, calls us to faith and conversion and sends us forward to share this gift with others. The wordless witnesses of Christian living will eventually prod some to inquire, "Why do you live as you do?" This is our opportunity for explicit proclamation, "Because I believe in Jesus and am trying to live as he taught."[11]

—) **T**he Gospel and Culture

Paul VI in *Evangelii Nuntiandi* emphasizes that the Church's mission is to evangelize culture. He states that "the split between the Gospel and culture is without a doubt the drama of our time:" and that "every effort must be made to ensure a full evangelization of culture, or more correctly, cultures" (20). He goes on to say that what really matters for the Church now "is to evangelize human culture (not in a purely decorative way as it were by applying a thin veneer, but a vital way, in depth, and right to their very roots)" (20).

The Synod for America expounded on this idea when they stated:

> It is important to evangelize persons individually and also to evangelize their cultures, since the goal is "a question not only of preaching the Gospel in ever wider geographic areas or to ever greater numbers of people, but also of affecting and as it were upsetting, through the power of the Gospel, mankind's criteria of judgment, determining values, points of interest, lines of thought, sources of

inspiration and models of life, which are in contrast with the word of God and the plan of salvation."[12]

That is, "what matters is to evangelize man's culture and cultures . . . in the wide and rich sense which these terms have in *Gaudium et Spes*."[13]

But since context and history are also essential features of human existence, culture is not monolithic; there is not one single culture, but a variety of cultures. This approach to evangelization has led to a new vocabulary in mission theology that includes such terms as *enculturation, acculturation,* and *inculturation.* Thus, we find in *Redemptoris Missio* that through inculturation,

> the church makes the Gospel incarnate in different cultures and at the same time introduces peoples, together with their cultures, into her own community. She transmits to them her own values, at the same time taking the good elements that already exist in them and renewing them from within. (52)

What is at stake when the Church is called to insert itself into the contemporary cultures of six continents (North and South America, Europe, Asia, Africa, and the Pacific)? This insertion process called *inculturation* first made its appearance in the 1977 international Synod of Bishops and further manifested itself in *Catechesis Tradendae* (1979), *Familiaris Consortio* (1981), and *Slavorum Apostoli* (1985). Inculturation has been defined as "the process of a deep, sympathetic adaptation to and appropriation of a local cultural setting in which the Church finds itself in a way that does not compromise its basic faith in Christ."[14]

But why speak of inculturation today? Three key reasons come to mind. First, individual cultures are coming to a new and enriched appreciation of their unique customs and traditions. These customs and traditions have been bases for their identity and the foundation of community life. As the Church grows in respectful appreciation of the All Holy's revelation in their history, space, and time, she seeks ways to cultivate bridges for understanding and reflecting upon the Gospel within their particular cultural context. Second, we are in an age of mission that challenges the Church to proclaim the Gospel in a rapidly changing technological world. Third, we are in an age of global awareness that includes the awareness of cultural diversity. The mass media are making us more aware of the rich and basic differences that exist between cultures. We realize that the new religious panorama requires a new perspective for introducing and planting the Good News in diverse cultures.

Recent studies in education, sociology, and psychology have demonstrated that peoples and cultures are different. The young child has different questions, outlooks, and needs from those of the aging. We know that men view life and its problems and possibilities differently than women do. The experiences of the Church in Asia, Africa, Latin America, the Caribbean, the Pacific, and North America are different. Each situation calls for a new way of being Church in each of their cultural contexts. It is within this pluralistic world that the Gospel is to be lived and proclaimed as being "fully alive" and meaningful to each particular context. There must be an existential fit. This is needed if an authentic "Amen; I believe, I accept discipleship" is to be clearly articulated and rooted into the lifeblood of the culture. The question of unity in diversity is always our challenge. Yet, the richness of the global diversity demands that if evangelization is to occur the diversity is to be appreciated and woven into our evangelization efforts.

Pope John Paul II, speaking to the African bishops assembled in Nairobi, Kenya, in 1980, stated:

> By respecting, preserving, and fostering the particular values and richness of your people's cultural heritage, you will be in a better position to lead them to a better understanding of the mystery of Christ, which is to be lived in the noble, concrete, and daily experience of African life. . . . It is a question of bringing Christ into the very center of African life, and lifting up all African life to Christ. Thus not only is Christianity relevant to Africa, but Christ in the members of his body is himself African.[15]

To gain some perspective on the issue of inculturation, on why it has emerged as a new imperative for the Church today, Avery Dulles reflects on H. Richard Niebuhr's classic study *Christ and Culture*. He streamlines Niebuhr's typology into three basic types: a confrontation model, a synthesis model, and transformation model.[16]

The confrontation model creates an opposition between Christianity and culture. This model is reflected in some modern Protestant theology, such as the thinking of Karl Barth who states that Christianity and culture must always be in conflict.[17]

Yet, how can one proclaim the Gospel without at least provisionally accepting the language and other cultural forms in which one is framing the message?[18] The reality of interrelationship between communication and culture becomes paramount in our discussion.

In the synthesis model culture is regarded as good in its own order, offering Christianity a suitable cultural base for evangelization. This is demonstrated by the Eurocentric mentality of Christianity that dominated the evangelization efforts of the Church over the centuries. In more recent times, the identification of Christianity with European culture has come to be perceived by some as a form of cultural imperialism and has provoked hostile reactions in Asia, Africa, Latin America, and some communities within the United States.[19]

The transformation model is more in tune with the Second Vatican Council and the spirit of the documents flowing from the council. It is a balance of the previous two. Avery Dulles identifies five points of the transformationist position:

1. In a certain sense, Christianity is supracultural.
2. Christianity has always been, and must be, culturally embodied.
3. Culture is broader than Christianity or any religion.
4. Christianity is not exclusively linked to any one culture.
5. The evangelization of cultures pertains to the mission of the Church.

This transformation model encourages evangelists, communicators, missionaries, and theologians to reach that naked *kenosis* (or emptying of one's self), the mystical core, and the supernatural faith that can be incarnated in any human culture. While the Gospel is compatible with all cultures, it poses a challenge to every culture and demands *metanoia,* conversion. Evangelization means the intimate transformation of authentic cultural values through their integration in Christianity in a process of inculturation. Paul VI, in his address to the African bishops, described this process.

The expression, that is, the language and mode of manifesting this one Faith, may be manifold; hence, it may be original, suited to the tongue, the style, the genius, and the culture, of the one who professes this one Faith. From this point of view, certain pluralism is not only legitimate, but also desirable. An adaptation of the Christian life in the fields of pastoral, ritual, didactic and spiritual activities is not only possible; it is even favored by the Church. The liturgical renewal is a living example of this. And in this sense you may, and you must, have an African Christianity. Indeed, you possess human values and characteristic forms of culture which can rise up to perfection such as to find in Christianity, and for Christianity, a true superior fullness, and prove to be capable of a richness of expression all its own, genuinely African. This may take time. It will require that your African soul become imbued to its depths with the secret charisms of Christianity, so that these charisms may then overflow freely, in beauty and wisdom, in the true African manner.[20]

A number of Asian and African Catholic theologians have been attempting to open new doors for identifying a more discerning way for Christianity to be communicated in diverse cultures. Raimundo Panikkar repeatedly calls our attention to the fundamental idea that the Christian event is seen as a supracultural fact. If until now it has adopted and adapted a certain garb, this is due to historical contingencies and/or the predominance of a particular culture over others. But, in itself, nothing stands in the way of Christianity taking flesh in the most remote and, for Western tastes, most exotic cultures.[21] Archbishop Ikenaga, during the Synod for Asia, stated:

> Asian people, influenced by European and American ways, have learned to take an intellectual and logical approach in announcing Truth. But in his heart the Asian places great importance on the body, on existence, on what is practical, on ontological expressions and symbols. From now on, be it in our talks on faith or the evangelization of society, in order to convey firmly the heart of Christianity we must use Asian ways of expression if our message is to take hold as we respond to the need to proclaim the Kingdom of God.[22]

During the 1990 Unda/OCIC World Congress in Bangkok, Thailand, the Catholic Church of Thailand shared the way video is used for evangelization and dialogue within their culture. Water was one of the integrating symbols used. Beginning with the Thai and Buddhist symbolic understanding of water, the video presentation created a bridge in drawing on the strengths of the prevailing culture to explain the meaning of baptism and reconciliation in the Christian tradition. Such an approach respects the traditions of the culture while speaking in the symbolic language of the people.

The symbolic representation of a Thai purification ritual was one of the highlights of the Congress. At the beginning and the end of the Buddhist season of Lent (Kao Pan Xa and Ock Pan Xa)—the special time of purification and of religious training in the Buddhist tradition—the people (in particular, the young people) prepare, with great devotion, bamboo sailboats covered with white paper. On the white paper, the people write their confessions, their promises, and their wishes. On the sides of the boat and on the mast, they place, in order and in line, white lighted candles. At nightfall, when a temple gong or drum signals the monks raising the prayer of Sayathro (the prayer of blessing) the boats, all lighted, are sailed down the river. The people applaud, cry aloud, and pray in thanksgiving. As our Congress moved in procession down to the river to float our candles, we discussed at length how rich this symbolism is for our Christian understanding of baptism and reconciliation.

In *Christianity Rediscovered,* Vincent Donovan shares with us his experience of missiology and evangelization among the Masai in Africa. Initially he approached his missionary work with his Western mentality well fixed and directed. Over time he learned to trust the cultural experience of the Masai and the translation of the Word by the wisdom figures within the community.

> And there was almost always a man in each community who was notably eloquent. He always had been eloquent, and was frequently called on by the community for speeches. He was their preacher. And every community had one or two people who had the power to take old and familiar things and make them new and challenging, to stir the people to action, to make them move when moving could be the difference between life and death in a nomadic community. We would have a name for those persons. We would call them prophets.

Donovan continues:

> Even before baptism I could see a pattern forming, a community of faith in the making, but not exactly the pattern of Christian community that I, from my background, had expected, or to which I was

accustomed. All I would add to that already formed pagan community was the dimension of faith, and on the reception of baptism they would become, as they were and where they were, a fully formed and functional church.[23]

—) The Challenge of the Media Age

The new media culture enables us to connect with the rich and varied cultures we have been speaking about so far. We can listen to their stories of conversion and faith through the media even while we are thousands of miles away. We can learn from their methods of inculturation how the Good News begins to vibrate through the life of their faith community. While advanced communications technologies may not be the means of their communication, the resources they use have meaning and impact. Yet, as we journey to various parts of the world, we already see the rapid expansion of the integration of modern means of communication in the smallest African, Oceanic, or Caribbean communities. No culture is being left untouched by the expansion of the new media age.

The exploding media realities are sensed as both a gift and a threat. We can either see them as gifts, evoking a call to use them creatively and innovatively for our ministry, or as a threat provoking the fear that media are too much of a distraction for hearing the Good News within our everyday lives. The new infomedia technologies have created new spaces and new contexts for the emerging new virtual and cybercommunities of faith. This can be perceived as a gift! As more and more people spend quality time in cyberspace, why shouldn't the Church, the local parish, position herself in cyberspace offering the cybergroups knowledge and an experience of the Gospel message?

This is being accomplished in a variety of ways today. Pastors are establishing online discussion lists to connect directly with their parishioners, especially the young adults who move away to the university to study. Many a pastor has spoken of his ongoing communication with these young people via the parish Web site and personal e-mail. Parish ministers speak about youth projects on the Internet bringing their young adults into dialogue on social justice and human rights issues through virtual communities designed and facilitated by the youth themselves. Thus, the social Gospel finds a new form of expression and enlightenment via the Internet.

Our own experience of designing courses on scripture, liturgy, Church leadership formation, and related topics has already begun to form a community of catechetics in cyberspace. This community is both national and international. We have participants from Singapore, the Philippines, Germany, and the Caribbean joining our cybercluster of catechists. As we continue to market—to announce—our cyber-courses via the search engines of the Internet and traditional print market techniques, our cybercommunity grows. In light of these few experiences, the media reality is perceived as a gift for new means of proclaiming and positioning the Good News in the cyberculture.

Furthermore, those of us who are producers of religious radio, television, and cable television programs know that marketing our programs is essential if they are to find a place within the public forum of the media landscape. Mass media airtime is not free in many, perhaps most, of our countries. We must purchase the airtime in order to broadcast our Gospel stories and messages into the homes of our audience. However, it is not only a matter of purchasing the airtime, we must also market our program so that our intended audiences will "become aware" that we exist within the media landscape. Thus, posters, billboards, newspaper ads, news releases, radio and TV spots may all become a way to announce the existence of the religious pro-gram that is our evangelization and catechesis in the public forum.

We understand the other side of the coin as well. There are many today who only perceive the media realities as a fear-provoking threat. There is a fear that the Gospel will be perceived as just anoth-er product on sale in today's intellectual and spiritual marketplace.[24] This perspective could be interpreted as meaning that there is no redemptive value in the media. The media by its very nature is dis-tracting, manipulative, and oppressive both to being human and for proclaiming the Gospel.

We experience the bombardment of images, sounds, and words through the bursting new communication technologies that screeches out to capture the imagination of people today. No matter where we turn we see images, words, and sounds embracing us. We encourage you to think about the following idea for one moment. What and where are the images, words, and sounds that embrace me everyday from the time I awake to the time I retire to my bed at night? In one form or another these new infomedia realities provoke a type of marketing or stimulation that is demanding on our senses.

Self-discipline within this new Infomedia cultural context is not easy. This is especially the case when we find ourselves in any public place over which we have no control. Consider airports, shopping centers, the workplace, doctor's offices, and other waiting rooms in which we find ourselves that continually insert the media messages into our lives. Another good example, and one that absolutely irritates me, is going to the cinema now and having ten to fifteen minutes of advertising bombarding me before the film begins. There are times I want to scream out (and I have already done this) and say, "I didn't pay to come to hear and see this. I want my money back!" Yes, this is the other side of the coin, on which infomedia can be seen as a threat and fear in our lives.

In the past the messenger and message may have been more controlled and defined. As we have seen, this is not the case today. New marketing techniques have enabled messengers and messages to come at us from many angles of beliefs, values, and attitudes. Filtering out or confronting these messages and messengers is not an easy task, yes, I agree. Discernment is critical. We control the way we allow these bombardments of images, words, and sounds to influence us. These are skills we must teach our children and ourselves. However, all this does not mean that we must close our doors to this media landscape, especially if we are ministers of the Good News within an advancing new mediasphere.

We find ourselves caught up in the so-called "tyranny of either/or." We believe that we need to redeem the term *marketing*. This means to understand it with all its dimensions and perspectives. We should not limit our understanding of marketing to only a single way of interpreting and understanding its role within the Infomedia culture. We acknowledge that the Infomedia culture has bright and shadow sides. How we engage in the development (design), formation (production), growth (expansion), and integration of the Infomedia culture into our lives is a challenge we cannot ignore.

We live in a historical moment when the media are changing their nature and extending their range. The changes have been building through the twentieth century, as the spoken word reanimated communication over telephone and radio, and as the moving image on film and television supplemented the "mere" word.[25] The invention and dissemination of the personal computer and now the explosive growth in links between those computers on the worldwide networks of the Internet create a genuinely new and transformative environment for proclaiming the Good News. We need to understand the depth and breadth of the meaning of marketing within this new environment. We cannot limit our interpretation only to the narrow popular sense of "buying and selling." We can be the designers and producers of an alternative message reflecting the Good News within the culture of the mass media and infomedia. For either with us or without us, this new Infomedia culture is going to expand with quantum leaps into the future.

The challenge we—the Church and its ministers—have before us is how are we to position the Gospel (what I now call mission-based marketing) within these diverse media contexts of radio, television, Internet, press, advertising, and so on. How is it that the Good News can vibrate as an alternative to the pluralistic religious and secular dimensions surrounding us?

While I will speak more about "mission-based marketing" in an upcoming chapter I will clarify it a bit here. Marketing, to our understanding, is a process for building responsiveness into our parish ministries. While the word *marketing* can and also does carry a lot of consumeristic baggage, there are some redeeming qualities to the concept. In the end, we may have to invent a new word for the "new reality" that we are attempting to create here. Thus, we may desire to use alternative terms for *marketing,* such as "announcing," "positioning," or imaging the Gospel in today's intellectual and spiritual marketplace.

St. Paul himself faced this challenge many times along his journeys. As we know from the Pauline letters, Paul was passionate about positioning the Good News about Jesus within the marketplace. He devoted a great deal of time and energy to the metropolitan centers of his time and to centering himself within the public forum—the gathering place of the masses. It was here that he preached. In Romans 10:14 we read: "But how are they to call upon one in whom they have not believed? And how are they to believe in one of whom they have never heard? And how are they to hear without someone to proclaim him?"

As indicated above, there are many dimensions and perspectives for really understanding the concept of mission-based marketing in our mass media world today. Mary Catherine Hilkert in defining preaching states: "The Hebrew *dabhar,* meaning 'to drive forward' or 'to push,' conveys a clear sense of energy, derived from the biblical understanding that the power of the word carries the power of its speaker."[26] In one sense, preaching is an expression of mission-based marketing. St. Paul stood amidst the public forum to proclaim his word among the many other images, sounds, and messages swirling around him. He frequently used ideas and experiences familiar to his audiences to capture their religious imagination in order to focus their attention on the message of Jesus.

Parish and Church leaders and ministers are seeking ways to communicate what is happening within the local church and/or world church and passionately hoping for an active response. We are finding that the traditional ways of announcing our messages are not having impact. Einstein is quoted as saying: "Do you know what absolute madness is? It is doing the same thing over and over and over again expecting different results!" We believe this is what happens in our parishes today. We continue to communicate in traditional ways and few people are listening to us. But do we change our ways? No, we keep right on going, throwing the blame on the listeners and forgetting about the methodology and/or techniques of the communicators.

Our young people are voting with their feet and moving out of parish and church life as they discover that the delivery of the message is becoming irrelevant and not meaningful in their lives. Note— we are not saying the "message" but the "delivery of the message." Delivery means a lot; it is how the message is packaged! How we package the message is mission-based marketing. It has to do with capturing the attention and/or the imagination of our intended audiences amidst the many packages displayed before them. The presentation or the packaging of the Good News of Jesus is imperative today. We firmly believe it is not the message that is obsolete, but the way it is being delivered.

—) **Q**uestions for Reflection

1. Consider a story of how the fourfold approach for evangelization described in this chapter has been demonstrated in your life. Can you pinpoint the four movements?

2. Reflect on the three questions from *Evangelii Nuntiandi*. What invitation and challenge emerge for your life and your parish?

3. Reflect on peak moments in your life when God broke through. Did the encounter result in some form of transformation? How did it express itself? What was its impact?

4. How might you use your God encounter story to spark an awareness or openness in the life of another person?

5. What new insights do you receive as you reflect on various cultures' experience and communication of their faith as described in this chapter?

Speaking About the Gospel and Marketing

Effective evangelization in the new religious
panorama requires a mission-based
marketing approach.

If we believe that the Spirit of the Lord calls all people and cultures
to their own fresh and creative response to the Gospel, perhaps we
need to shake off the sluggishness of time past and allow our lives to
be reawakened with a "New Pentecost"! If we are living in a *kairos*
moment of history and the time has come to engage in a new evangelization and a new mission-based marketing technique, what is it
we are called to do?

──┤ **I**s There a Place for the Conversation?

There is a common assumption among many people that they can be
spiritual without the church, that they can follow their own conscience and develop their "personal faith" in a way that is uniquely
their own.[1] We have seen that spiritual seekers, fundamentalism, secularism, New Age spiritualities, faith syncretism, and similar trends
signal that Christianity is being challenged on many fronts. In light of
this new reality, Christians need to rethink our paradigms for "positioning" or "marketing" the Good News of Jesus. Is it impossible to
think in terms of marketing when speaking about the Gospel? In earlier chapters we discussed some of the resistance one receives as
soon as one speaks about "marketing" and the "Gospel" in the same

sentence. The term *marketing* does carry a lot of baggage. However, we believe there is something for us to learn about marketing. As we indicated in the last chapter, perhaps "mission-based marketing" is a better term. But, whatever we call it, we definitely need to find new ways to package the Good News in the new media age!

Perhaps one of the most significant developments of the late twentieth century has been that the assent to particular doctrines, creeds, teachings, and religious commitment has become problematic for many. In the not so recent past the assent to faith seemed so natural as it was woven into the fabric of family, neighborhood, village, and cultural life. One did not ask questions, for the particular religious reality was confirmed by the lifestyle and the structure of the local community.

The times have changed. We know that something new and different is sweeping around the world. It is impacting women, men, and children at all levels and places of their lives. We find that people today are not blindly loyal to the denominations in which they were raised, and they are not hesitant about testing different churches. It is imperative therefore that we take a good long look at expanding our traditional understanding of introducing, or positioning or marketing the Good News. Note we are not eliminating anything we have and are doing today. We need to expand our consciousness of proclaiming within a new context.

To the three "burning questions" from *Evangelii Nuntiandi* we discussed above, Paul VI added a fourth:

> Does the church or does she not find herself better equipped to proclaim the Gospel and to put it into people's hearts with conviction, freedom of spirit and effectiveness? (4)

These four questions are the stimuli and rationale for contemplating a new way of appreciating marketing the Good News. While there is no single answer, there are alternative approaches that may be considered in order to capture the religious imagination of women, men, and children today. What can and should be done in the early stages of the twenty-first century to bring about the changes the Church seeks in order to realize her mission of evangelization in the new mediasphere? A more comprehensive understanding of marketing may open the windows and doors for positioning the Good News in the new religious panorama of the world.

Marketing is a controversial word or concept to introduce into most religious arenas today. Yet, if we can come to terms with the basic principles of marketing we may find it has a relationship to our evangelization efforts. Marketing is not an end but rather a tool. Marketing is not selling, advertising, or promotion, though it may include all of these. Marketing is a process for making concrete decisions about what the Church can do, and cannot do, to realize her mission in a new era. Marketing enables us to design a process for building responsiveness to the diverse groups of spiritual seekers and their needs that are crying out to be addressed, met, and embraced in meaningful covenant ways.

Although she has not used the term, we find that the Church has been and continues to be marketing herself in rich and diverse ways. Most of the people who founded religious organizations and agencies were women and men who utilized some form of marketing to capture the imagination of the people within their cultural environment. Even John Paul II's journeys around the world are a form of mission-based marketing. Think of all the dimensions of marketing that have been part of his visits and presence in various countries.

There is no doubt in my mind that the message of the Good News is relevant to our world. The Good News has something profound to say to the people of our times. The problem is with how we are delivering the message to the contemporary culture. In one sense the Church has lost sensitivity and touch with the people she serves. The synods of recent years have been articulating this fact and are attempting to come to grips with this reality. Keeping in mind that we wish to avoid the "tyranny of either/or" whereby one mode of evangelization is preferred to the exclusion of others, we see that a vibrant understanding and appreciation of marketing is critical if the effectiveness called for by Paul VI is to be realized.

The first place to begin is in rethinking our attitudes about marketing in general. There are many levels to marketing. While not all elements of marketing may have relevance to our missionary activities we should not reject them without careful deliberation. The "new methods" called for in *Evangelii Nuntiandi* may be rooted in what is called mission-based marketing.[2] However, before we examine mission-based marketing, let's consider marketing in general as it may relate to our evangelization efforts.

Marketing has been stigmatized because it is associated with the many frustrations of wanting and giving—with material things and guilt over the desire for them. Yet selling is only one of many functions of marketing. Marketing grows out of the essential quest to serve human needs. Marketing helps to communicate and persuade people of the worth of religious experience, and to demonstrate the value of religion in their lives and of the beneficial consequences of their active involvement with the Good News and/or the Church. Marketing for the Church is concerned with changing not the content but the process. This is an important point. Marketing skills are an essential element of ministry formation in order for individuals in ministry to understand and respond to the changing religious panorama today. In one sense it is an attempt to understand our audience. Who are they? Where are they? What is their spiritual quest? What are their needs? How is it that the Good News may speak in ways that are relevant but rooted in tradition? What language, psychology, and techniques will assist in our evangelization efforts? These are marketing questions and concerns!

In seeking ways to address these questions we do not imply that one's theology should be adjusted to meet the market or audience demand. We do mean that the process by which a Church or parish presents the Good News and doctrine should be developed by considering the prospective recipients' perspective, rather than the evangelizer's perspective, on what is needed or of value at a particular moment.[3]

Those who are engaged in the evangelizing process need to walk gently into the culture and/or experience of others respecting what already is present in their lives. Aylward Shorter uses a good term, "threshold dialogue" to describe this idea. He states:

> This is the approach in which Christians experience the way people of other traditions live their culture and religion. They cross another's threshold, as it were, and, after such an experience, reflect upon it in the light of their own Christian faith. An encounter takes place, therefore, not at a conference table, but within the heart and conscience of Christians.[4]

Here the experience of the profound mystery of the presence of God is being revealed. The evangelizer must respect this threshold dialogue as an experience of ongoing revelation. He or she prepares the way and the Spirit is the one who touches the mind and heart of the individual to be receptive to the Event!

In one sense, we need to reflect on an idea that was proposed in *To Kill a Mockingbird*. Atticus is attempting to help his children understand how important it is to comprehend the diverse experiences of people within their culture. He says, "You must learn to walk in their shoes." Walking in another's shoes is an endeavor to arrive at an epiphany of understanding the mindset of the other person. How can we evangelize unless we understand the other as other with his or her richness, diversity, and questions? What is required is "outside-in" thinking, not "inside-out" thinking. While rooted in the message and our mission we must endeavor to reach out to others in our evangelization initiatives by beginning where our audience is. This is mission-based marketing!

Two traditional methodological principles can guide our acknowledgment for mission-based marketing for evangelization: adaptation and apperception. Adaptation is basic to all evangelization and Catechetical ministry. It states that good teaching is adapted to the maturation and needs of the student. Apperception is rooted in the fact that knowledge is a living growth and it proceeds from the known to the unknown. Apperception is a technique that enables the catechist or evangelizer to demonstrate connectedness between existing knowledge and experience with the new knowledge and experience of the Gospel.[5]

St. Paul is an excellent model for applying adaptation and apperception to his missionary activities. Where did Paul proclaim the message of Jesus? He did not limit himself to the synagogues. We read in the Acts of the Apostles that he went daily to the public square and he preached to whoever happened to be there (Acts 17:17). He spent significant amounts of time in the marketplace adapting his message to his audience (Acts 17:22). He sought out images and words that were familiar to the peoples of Corinth, Ephesus, Thessalonica, the islands, and his entire journey through Asia Minor. He knew that he needed to make a connection to capture the religious imagination of the people to awaken them to the message and meaning of the Good News. Like Jesus, Paul used every means in the marketplace to point the way and implant the message. We should be doing the same in the new mediasphere.

—) **M**ission-Based Marketing

This brings us back to our earlier point concerning mission-based marketing. Peter Brinckerhoff uses this term for nonprofit organizations. He believes that nonprofit marketing is about prompting individuals or groups to take, or to abandon, specific action. Is this not what conversion is all about? Rebecca Leet elaborates on this, stating that for Brinckerhoff the key words are marketing and mission—not marketing and fund-raising, not marketing and public relations, not marketing and direct mail, not marketing and membership recruitment.[6] She indicates that nonprofit marketing is more complex and more difficult than its for-profit counterpart. She refers to Gary Stern, a nonprofit marketing trainer, who defines marketing for the nonprofit sector of society: Marketing is a process that helps you exchange something of value for something you need. Or another: "Marketing helps you identify those people who are most likely to want to exchange with you and helps you understand what they want from their relationship with you."[7] Leet tries to help us understand that mission-based marketing is a "business philosophy, a way of thinking, an orientation to an organization's total activities." She goes on to say that a nonprofit that employs mission-based marketing changes the way it identifies needs, conducts planning, solves problems, and evaluates success.

Effective evangelization in the new religious panorama requires a mission-based marketing approach. How do we adopt such an approach? First, the primary focus is on the audience. What is it that individuals are seeking today? How is their desire consistent with the mission of the Church or religious organization? It means we need to redirect our thinking from what we think the audience or individual may need to what they want. Second, to determine what our audience wants we must be ready to ask. And, third, the success of mission-based marketing is focusing on our target audience or our niche. Niche marketing means designing marketing programs so that they are specifically tailored to a select audience that has been carefully identified. Listening and responding are elements essential to mission-based marketing.

An immediate example comes to mind. Several years ago a pastor contacted our center to design and plan a Lenten Adult Religious Education series for the parish. He had several concerns: (1) adults were not participating in adult religious education programs in the parish; (2) adults needed to have a deeper understanding of the Catholic faith; and (3) adults needed to be more active in parish life. With these concerns before us I met with his parish council. We discussed what they were looking for and how they anticipated their goal would be realized. The goal was a Lenten Adult Religious Education Lecture Series. Even though the educational history of the parish indicated few adults were coming out for the adult religious education programs, the group was rooted in their original paradigm of adult religious education. How could we help them realize their mission while shifting the paradigm?

The basic principle of Malcolm Knowles, a well-known adult education philosopher, is, "adults only come out for that which they perceive they need." Working from this principle, we decided to ask the parishioners what information would motivate them to participate in an adult lecture series. One Sunday we handed out 5" x 8" cards to all the parishioners before the Liturgy, asking them to prioritize the topics that were of interest and or value for themselves today. The list included scripture, doctrine, the Ten Commandments, prayer, family issues and concerns, Gospel values. Space was provided for individuals to suggest on additional areas. Of a possible 1,600 returns we received 850 by the end of the day. This is an excellent result. What do you think were the choices of the parishioners? Well, family issues and concerns were number one on the list, with prayer and Gospel values close behind. Thus, we designed a six-week series around Catholic Christian Family Issues and Concerns. The topics included Family and Adolescent Communication, Family and Care for Elderly Parents, the Ten Commandments, Family and Conflict, Values in the Contemporary World, and Family and Spirituality.

You may be wondering how the Ten Commandments came to be on the list. When the pastor studied the design and themes of the lecture series he was disappointed. Where were the Church's teachings? "These must be explicit!" he stated. We indicated that the series was based upon the indicators of interest (mission-based marketing) listed by his parishioners on Sunday. We assured him that the Church teachings would be included in the presentations but the focus would meet the adults where they perceived they had needs. Nonetheless, we compromised a bit by including his Ten Commandments in the list.

Finally the Lenten series began. It is important to know that in the past ten years only fifteen to twenty parishioners had participated in the series. This was one of the reasons for the pastor's concern for a program that would, as he said, "make a difference." What he had to realize was that the difference might not be what he expected. We tried to assure him that the parishioners, the audience, needed to feel connected and motivated by the themes as it related to their immediate needs. The first session drew 250 people, the second 345 people and it continued to grow until we reached the next-to-last session: "The Ten Commandments." The attendance dropped to about 50! The rapidly advancing enthusiasm of the pastor was deflated with the drop in number to 50! "What happened?" he queried. "We were doing so well! This is what they really needed." Perhaps they did, but not now! The parishioners perceived a more urgent need—family. In the last session the numbers were back up to 345. Well, numbers may not be all that important. Yet, the realities demonstrated that mission-based marketing is effective. This same principle needs to be applied to any media or Internet program or experience we attempt to create. Programs and experiences succeed or fall short of their mark depending on the integration of mission-based marketing into our planning process.

The starting point for change is where the audience is, and the pathway to change lies in providing what they feel they need, consistent with our mission. A mission-driven approach to marketing realizes that to make change we must orient our programs and messages to our audience because it is they who act or do. The pastor was concerned with needs. Whose needs were they? Brinckerhoff states that there is a difference between needs and wants. People have needs but people seek wants. So, the truth is, if we want people to change people must first want to change. You may take steps to create or increase the desire, but it must still be there. Thus, in attempting to explore ways to "break open the Word anew" we need to cultivate a mindset of mission-based marketing as one valued approach to ministry.

A mission-based marketing approach requires that the parish or religious organization systematically study needs, wants, perceptions, preferences, and satisfaction of the members or potential members that they are trying to reach. Since people and environments change, the parish or religious organization must adapt and customize its specific products or services and "packaging," while remaining faithful to its doctrine.[8] The perennial concern of Church leaders is the "watering-down or selling the message short" in a marketing forum. This does not have to be the case. The study and training of ministers in mission-based marketing can draw out the positive elements of marketing for our mission. The Church will more and more need to consider modern marketing practices because communicating the values of any religion is an increasingly "tough sell" in the new religious panorama.

The new mediasphere has enlarged our marketing and communication arenas for proclaiming the Good News. It has multiple opportunities for interpersonal encounters, giving those in remotest places access to sound and images from other places throughout the world. Expanding radio, television, cable, and the Internet along with ISDN systems, fiber optics and T 1–4 lines, multimedia CDs and DVDs have created a new mediasphere in which interactive networking among new delivery systems makes it possible to respond to hundreds of different needs, tastes, and interests within the religious panorama.[9] Ease of production and transmission is shifting the media landscape and our potential participation within it.

The new mediasphere leads to strikingly different communication behaviors in that they require a high degree of individual involvement. A person must actively select the information content that he or she wants. It further is causing an integration of media that we have conventionally considered to be completely separate. This is best exemplified by the converging of computers and telephones, the Internet with print, radio, and video and live synchronous interactivity anywhere at anytime in the world. We live in a new era—a new marketplace of the mediasphere. In this new mediasphere we must adjust and reposition our evangelization initiatives. While remaining true to the message of Jesus Christ we must embrace new languages, new psychology, and new techniques. What methods should be followed in order that the Power of the Gospel may have its effect? is a perennial question requiring us to shift our paradigms from a traditional approach to marketing the message to one that engages the full breadth and depth of the new mediasphere.

Karl Rahner's meditation on Advent inspires us to be a Church to open new possibilities and directions. He reminds us that we are a pilgrim people. We are a people moving forward, not standing still. He says, "Advent demands that we look to the future; we are a people of expectation and hope." He goes on to say that in Advent we should really ask ourselves in complete intimacy and concreteness if the spirit and heart in us still have a little room for novelty and future beyond the present."[10]

If we believe that the Spirit of the Lord calls all people and cultures to its own fresh and creative response to the Gospel, perhaps we need to shake off the sluggishness of time past and allow our lives to be reawakened with a "New Pentecost"! If we are living in a *kairos* moment of history and the time has come to engage in a new evangelization and a new mission-based marketing technique, what is it we are called to do?

—) **Q**uestions for Reflection

1. Is it possible to speak about "marketing" and the "Gospel" in the same breath? Why?
2. How does your parish (Church) position the Gospel in your community? What approaches are used? How effective are they?
3. What is impossible to do today in your parish (Church) to evangelize the people (culture), that if it could be done, would fundamentally change how we are church?
4. What is "Threshold Dialogue"? How might it be implemented in your parish?
5. How do you now understand "mission-based marketing"? How might your parish (Church) engage in it? Think about some practical models.

A New Portal
for the
"Good News"

The world is in great need of "imagineers" of the Gospel;
that is, individuals who are able to vision new patterns
and use new techniques (technologies) as the tools
of an artist to capture the religious
imagination of the culture.

People today are fascinated by the image, by what is visible and concrete rather than by reason or abstract knowledge. This means we have to rediscover the image dimension of the Gospel. Since the word that moves, attracts, and empowers people today is not an abstract doctrinal word but the word of story, metaphor, and image, we must recover that liberating word within all aspects of our religious experience.

How many of us suffer from the Rip Van Winkle syndrome? One day we awoke to discover the world had changed. There was a new culture with a new language, a new psychology, and new techniques for communication and information. What we traditionally understood by mouse, menu, navigation, cruising, surfing, netting had been replaced with new definitions. The language shifted even further with new concepts such as netizens, cyberzens, gigabytes, cyberspace, java, jazz, zip, virtual reality, virtual communities, telementoring, and telepresence.

We find that the meaning of "place" has changed. The classroom is no longer confined to four walls. The idea of global communities

of learning, decision making, and political, social, and religious discourse in cyberspace is becoming the common reality. As we attempt
to create a sense of equilibrium within this new culture, we discover
it will not stand still for us. It is fast, complex, compressed, multimedia, uncertain, and interactive. As soon as we seem to understand it,
it has shifted.

We try to comprehend how we are to communicate faith within
this new milieu. We wonder if it is possible that our traditional religious
language has lost its power of imagination in the contemporary world.
While some Church leaders and ministers attempt to hide, ignore, or
reject the technological evolution, others surrender, embrace, and
become advocates for the dawning of the new era. They understand
that the new reality will not disappear. In *To Teach as Jesus Did* we
read: "Technology is one of the most marvelous expressions . . . but it
is not an unmixed blessing . . . it can enrich life . . . or make a tragedy
of life. The choice is ours and education has a powerful role in shaping that choice" (#33). The challenge before us today is to be active participants in the formation of this new audiovisual, multimedia cyberculture. We are to become artisans of faith in cyberspace.

Bear in mind that with or without the Church this new culture will
continue to evolve at an unprecedented pace, weaving itself into the
fabric of our everyday lives. The Church throughout history has had
a rich tradition of embracing new techniques for evangelization via
the arts. However, at times the Church has lost opportunities because
of fear, reluctance, or lack of experimentation and vision. As we have
seen, the diverse profile of the existing religious panorama and its
expansion supported by the media and the Internet confirms we cannot assume such a posture today. The Church must advance with
Internet and cyberspace opportunities.

As we stand on the threshold of the twenty-first century, we must
be bold. Cyberspace is the new frontier. Are we willing to become
pioneers of faith within the new frontier? What new mindsets and
skills are required? What techniques (tools) are available for us within our parish, school, or local community? What new steps are
required for us to move forward? Recall Einstein's comment that:
"Absolute madness is doing the same thing over and over and over
again, expecting different results." Recognizing the importance and
need for change is a mark of a healthy, renewing Church.

—) The Emergence of New Paradigms: The Apostle Paul and Karl Rahner

Change is not a foreign idea to the Church. Once again consider St. Paul's situation in the early Church. His conversion and missionary activities brought a radical shift in how the early Church understood herself. The official turning point occurred at the Council of Jerusalem. The Acts of the Apostles gives us a glimpse of what may have been a very explosive and complicated conversation among the disciples. The original perception of whom the Church was to evangelize and the responsibilities of the evangelized to the Church were being shifted within the Gentile community. So, we read:

> Then certain individuals came down from Judea and they were teaching the brothers, "Unless you are circumcised according to the custom of Moses, you cannot be saved." And after Paul and Barnabas had no small dissension and debate with them, Paul and Barnabas and some of the others were appointed to go up to Jerusalem to discuss this question with the apostles and the elders. . . . When they came to Jerusalem, they were welcomed by the church and the apostles and the elders, and they reported all that God had done with them. But some believers who belonged to the sect of the Pharisees stood up and said, "It is necessary for them to be circumcised and ordered to keep the law of Moses." (Acts 15:1–5).

After much debate within the Council a resolution is reached. A new paradigm for evangelizing the Gentile world is defined. Paul and Barnabas are to be sent forth to pave the way for a new paradigm of evangelization.

The paradigm shift initiated by Paul's interpretation of his mission by the spirit unsettled the early Church. He fundamentally was changing the boundaries and the rules of how they understood "being and becoming Church" in their era. The paradigm shift was profound because it shifted the way the local Church imaged and communicated itself to Asia Minor. The shift resulted in a radical *metanoia* of various dimensions within the very life of the Church!

The Council of Jerusalem was not the only major paradigm shift the Church experienced in her history. Karl Rahner points out that the history of the Church speaks of constant change. The Church is a pilgrim people. The Church is a people on the move. Movement into new environments necessarily brings about a clash of experiences with some degree of adaptation. Rahner indicates that two other periods of history were as dramatic: first, the Reformation, and second, the Second Vatican Council. The Council of Jerusalem opened the Church's doors to the Gentile world in Asia Minor, the period following the Reformation wedged those doors further open as the perception of a world church intensified, and finally the Second Vatican Council explicated a world Church that was not only Western or European but a Church of rich cultural diversity. The experience and insights of the Apostle Paul and Rahner indicate that the Church's shifting of her paradigm is not an unfamiliar project. Yet, what is the reality of such a shift? What actually happens?

The procedure for shifting to a new paradigm, while traditionally a slow process, picked up momentum in the last quarter of the twentieth century. This accelerating movement is not a comfortable position for an organization or institution that approaches change with caution. Let's face it—in most circumstances, people begin to think about change only when they're in trouble, see trouble on the horizon, or see new creative opportunities before them. The reality is that new paradigms show up sooner than they are needed or wanted. Practitioners of a dominant paradigm have tied their time and their reputation and their success in life to the old paradigm so, of course, they feel they have everything to lose and almost nothing to gain by shifting their paradigm. Because paradigms act as perceptual filters through which we view the world, the idea or data that doesn't fit the roles of our paradigm has a hard time getting through our filters.[1]

This is how tension arises. What is perfectly obvious to a person with one paradigm may not be perceived at all by someone with a different paradigm. Old paradigms blind people to new opportunities. Since the new mediasphere is so radically different, if we desire to position our evangelization efforts within this sphere we must be ready to shift the paradigm of the way we evangelize today. As initiators of a new paradigm, we need to get outside the borders of our traditional thinking, break our own rules of past success, develop new reading habits, converse with innovators in the new culture, and have a good sense of humor with a lot of flexibility.

In *Tactics of Innovation* Barker indicates that it is not only a matter of the design and implementation of new ideas; the way we introduce the new idea or innovation into our ministry settings is also critical if a paradigm shift is to take effect. Church leaders, catechists, and evangelizers are concerned with how well the new idea or innovation will fit into their current environment of ministry. They are concerned also about the compatibility of the idea with what they are doing now and doing well. So, what tactics should we consider in order to bring about the desired shift in our introduction of evangelization and catechesis in the mediasphere? Barker give us several clues:

1. Individuals must see the idea's advantage over what they are already doing.

2. The smaller the negative consequences, the better the idea's initial acceptance.

3. The idea must appear simple from the point of view of the catechist, leader, or evangelizer, however complex it may seem from our own point of view.

4. The idea should be introduced in increments—remember, "It's a cinch by the inch but hard by the yard."

5. The message must be clearly presented in a language with which our catechists, leaders, and evangelizers are comfortable and familiar, without technical or theological jargon.

6. There must be an "existential fit"; that is, the new idea must match up with what our catechists, leaders, and evangelizers are already using or experiencing.

7. The new idea or innovation must be credible and reliable.

8. There must be an "easy in" and "easy out"; that is, the new idea can be easily tried and easily abandoned if it does not work out.[2]

Architecture is a good metaphor for us to use as we think and discuss change in our Church, parishes, and ministries. Architects are concerned with the architecture of change, as well as with the architecture of stability.[3] Keeping our ministry efforts positioned within the new mediasphere requires the same effort that goes into painting a long bridge. By the time a crew has gone from one end to the other, it is usually time to start over on the original side and begin anew.

Seasoned designers and rebuilders know how difficult it is to change just one thing. Moving just one wall may involve a dozen other structural and infrastructural changes. Thus, change is an ongoing process affecting every dimension of the system. If we have skilled tactics in place, we may be able to nurture acceptance of the new idea(s) or innovation(s) that will influence the new architecture of evangelization in the new mediasphere.

—) The Signaling of Twenty-First–Century Shifts

The impact of the expansion forces us to understand new ways of being Church today within this rich cultural diversity, as reflected in the outcomes of the Synods for Africa, Asia, Oceania, Europe, and the Americas.

Bishop Arturo Bastes has stated that shifts in perspective "have to be made so that the Asian church will truly emerge, and consequently the religious formation will have to be 'Asianized.'"[4] In his address during the Synod for Asia Bishop Bastes points out three major shifts which must occur within the Asian context: a shift in understanding history, a shift in Church model, and a shift in understanding spirituality. He points out that "Christianity itself was born in Asia, but it has been alienated from Asia because of the perspective of a Euro-centered church." The Catholic Bishops' Conference of the Philippines suggests that the Asian synod must "explore exhaustively in an open and humble way the revelatory nature of the religions of Asia and their impact on the church's proclamation of Jesus." In reference to a Church model, Bishop Bastes says "many local churches in the so-called Third World are striving to shift away from a triumphalistic model of the church to a church identified with the social conditions of the people. The model of the church of the poor is being adopted my many local Asian churches."[5] Finally, in reference to the shift in spirituality, "In our traditional Catholic way of looking at spirituality we associate it with an institutional way of living, either with the religious life or with the ordained ministry. It had been difficult to consider spirituality otherwise than associated with an institution or a religious order. We need to shift our understanding of spirituality from institutionalized spirituality to incarnational spirituality."

These ideas were reiterated copious times in the various interventions which were made by Bishops during the Synod for Asia. Archbishop Ikenago further stretched the new paradigm being recommended when he said:

> The God of Christianity is limitless and possesses both fatherly and motherly elements. However, the Christianity that came from Europe tends to overstress the former. In the East we need to give greater expression to the feminine aspects of God: God who permeates the universe, lives in us through faith, receives all people in his embrace, the God of universal love, infinite tenderness, always ready to forgive, Christ atoning for all the sins of mankind on the Cross. If our theology, art, preaching and evangelization move along these lines, then Christianity will take on a gentler, more approachable face for Asian people.[6]

Aylward Shorter in writing on *Christianity and the African Imagination* expounds on paradigm shifts that must occur within the African context if evangelization is to be effective.[7] He points out that African theology must strike out on its own and use a method that is in accord with is own cultural form. He calls upon a narrative theology and the abandonment of the metaphysical abstractions traditionally applied to theology. He perceives that African traditional religious thought "is closer to Newman's 'first order language,' to the primary symbols of oral tradition, and therefore, to the language of faith." He teases the idea further by holding that if African theology were to become the "heir of Africa's oral culture—the co-heir with African creative writing—there is a chance that it might be taken more seriously, and that it would not be confused with the purposes and methods of Western theology."[8]

In each of these instances we see the local Church trying to adapt and adjust its paradigm for more effective evangelization approaches and techniques. The Spirit of these synods has been released and we now experience the dawning of a new era for evangelization.

The new mediasphere is another new global culture that the Church must come to terms with in her evangelization efforts. Here also the Church must shift her paradigm for effective evangelization in the twenty-first century. The role of the evangelizer today is one that must recognize that "modern society increasingly defines itself by communication . . . [the Church] asks once again how she can image and echo God in this world."[9]

⎯) The New Media Landscape: Cyberspace

Changes in the communications media have always had vast repercussions on the Church's understanding of its own nature and mission. Church structures and theology were radically transformed by the transitions from oral to manuscript culture and from manuscript culture to the age of print. The infomedia revolution through which we are passing is fully as radical as that of any other period. We have come to see that the new infomedia are influencing a new world and triggering a new human consciousness.

The world is in great need of "imagineers" of the Gospel; that is, individuals who are able to vision new patterns and use new techniques (technologies) as the tools of an artist to capture the religious imagination of the culture. Recently I read a book entitled *The Disney Way*. The book highlights what enabled Walt Disney to capture the "imagination" not only of the culture but also of the people with whom he surrounded himself. He began by forming a group of people he called "imagineers." Their job is to be engaged in "imagineering"; that is, to engage in constant creative thinking about the work they are missioned to do. Today, there are approximately 2,000 imagineers at the five Disney sites.[10] Imagine what could happen if we applied this principle of "imagineering" to the communication and evangelization ministry of the Church!

In order to maintain the "imagineering" spirit employees are encouraged to participate in "Dream Retreats." The Dream Retreat methodology is, "If you can Dream it, you can Do it." A Dream Retreat has proved to be an ideal way of helping people initiate needed change. Besides involving employees in strategy and facilitating their understanding of the vision and direction the company is pursuing, a Dream Retreat environment propels participants into a world of new ideas that often spark innovative solutions to the problems at hand. People who have been engaged in a "Dream Retreat" have discovered that it increases the opportunities for figuring out what's needed early in the process before one spends a lot of time reworking a change. Walt Disney had a four-pillared philosophy to bring his ideas into reality: Dream, Believe, Dare, and Do! Furthermore, Walt Disney instinctively knew that participation by all the workers in the development of a new idea gave them a sense of commitment, both to the idea in question and to the company itself.

I am not suggesting that as Church that we need to totally accept the "Disney Way" for our ministry. However, I do believe there are some worthwhile things we can learn from Disney. It is all too easy to think within the box. We may wish to ensure that what we have been doing in the past will continue to be the same. We need to put "new wine into new wineskins" if a dramatically new evangelization and communications reality is to make a difference in our world through proclaiming the Good News.

This Disney idea does affect how we could re-contemplate our evangelization ministry especially in the light of the new communication technologies. In *Communio et Progressio* we read: "The People of God walk in history. As they . . . advance with their times, they look forward with confidence and even enthusiasm to whatever the development of the communications age may offer" (#187). People today are fascinated by the image, by what is visible and concrete rather than by reason or abstract knowledge. This means we have to rediscover the image dimension of the Gospel. Since the word that moves, attracts, and empowers people today is not an abstract doctrinal word but the word of story, metaphor, and image, we must recover that liberating word within all aspects of our religious experience.

Catechists and evangelizers need to identify new perspectives and possibilities (new paradigms) for retelling the stories of Scripture within the human stories of today or, alternatively, for disclosing the spirituality of the human situation in the light of scripture. Such storytelling may take the form of narrowcasting, reaching out to a more defined, specialized audience, for example through low-power radio, cable TV, videocassettes, DVD, CDs, or group media. Broadcasting (national or regional radio, television, the Internet or WebTV) offers the Church an opportunity for reaching mass audiences throughout the culture. There is also the opportunity to design interactive multimedia experiences via computers, computer software, personally produced and pressed CDs, DVDs, and to navigate through the rapidly growing avenues of cyberspace. We know already from our continuous navigation and research in cyberspace that "virtual communities of faith" are mushrooming in cyberspace!

So, where do we begin? We can start "tinkering around"! Tinkers make do with the materials at hand, opening new possibilities by experimenting and playing around with ideas. They respect and accept the traditional means of communication but are receptive to new avenues and visions. While, radio, television, print, and film continue to be worthy avenues of support for our evangelization initiative, we will focus on the new role of computers, the Internet, and cyberspace. Evangelizers, catechists, and ministers are called to invest more time and attention in experimentation with the exploding culture of the Internet for proclaiming and positioning the Gospel within today's cyberculture.

History suggests that a new communication medium tends to complement rather than replace other media. Although the Internet is currently the latest, hottest medium (largely because of the World Wide Web), it will not only continue to coexist but will converge with other media in the coming years. The continued need for print materials about the Internet is demonstrated by the many print newsletters and magazines fueled by the growth of the Internet—*Internet World, Web Developer, Wired,* and countless others. It is also notable that the fastest growing section in our local bookstore consists of books about the World Wide Web and Internet. This is a good example of the ways in which media often reinforce each other.

Profile and Expansion of Cyberspace

The combination of computers, the Internet, and cyberspace is the single phenomenon of the past decade that is revolutionizing our lives. Offering incredible capacities and speed for data collection, analysis, and dissemination, this expanding new technology and new "place" is ushering in a new age. It is transforming our communication patterns, the work we do, and our leisure time.[11] Indeed, as recently as twenty years ago the term "computer literacy" might have been reserved to business and government. Today computer, digital, and Internet literacy are paramount for education, leisure, and family communication, as well as for positioning the Good News within the vastly expanding virtual communities in cyberspace. This culture is expanding! In 1998 there were over one hundred million people using e-mail, over one million home pages and Web sites—and the numbers continue to grow every day on every continent.

Those who have learned to navigate through the vast reaches of cyberspace find on the Internet an astonishing variety of conversations taking place daily, a tropical greenhouse of discourse communities in bloom, a laboratory of extended conversations and social experiments organized around every conceivable topic and interest. Just as we are beginning to feel comfortable with word processing, personal computers, and basic Internet capabilities with e-mail, electronic data exchanges, and global telecommunications networks, a new and even stronger electronic horizon is beckoning: the invisible but intense world of cyberspace. Today's e-mail may be the port of entry into cyberspace, but it barely hints at what is there.

The world's expanding digital infrastructure will open up a whole New World of opportunities and challenges that test the imagination. A place must be cleared within this new cyberculture for the preaching of the Gospel. Cyberspace is neither a fad nor science fiction. Cyberspace is a metaphor because it identifies the region where electronic communication occurs as being a kind of space. The science fiction writer Bruce Sterling refers to cyberspace as not exactly "real" but nevertheless a genuine place where things happen that have actual consequences: careers are made in cyberspace, thieves prowl in cyberspace, increasingly complete records of our lives are stored in cyberspace. Cyberspace is a rapidly growing new cultural space with diverse creeds, codes, and cults. Cyberspace culture is not passive but interactive.

Cyberspace represents a subtle but profound paradigm shift in the nature of communications. The topography of this landscape is represented by a variety of graphic interfaces that help orient those who explore it. Electronic archives and libraries store documents and record transactions; threads of conversations persist—in groups and in the minds of individual participants.[12] It is without geographic features in the ordinary sense. It is a communications space—a virtual space in which people will spend even more of their lives teaching, learning, meeting colleagues, organizing their work, home, and leisure lives, carrying on idle or serious conversations, and searching for religious meaning and experiences.

If the Internet is truly forming a culture, or a complex of cultures, it should not surprise us that as more people come to spend more and more of their time online, they have begun to devise ways to fulfill the religious needs and identities that form such an important part of the fabric of our society. In a 1990 address entitled "The Church Must Learn to Cope with Computer Culture," John Paul II noted the revolutionary impact of contemporary developments in communication such as cyberspace: "One no longer thinks or speaks of social communications as mere instruments or technologies. Rather they are now seen as part of a still unfolding culture whose full implications are yet imperfectly understood and whose potentialities remain for the moment only partially exploited." The mandate for those in ministry, evangelization, and leadership therefore requires keeping abreast of the growing new reality of computers, the Internet, and cyberspace. Since this reality is expanding at quantum speed the Church must maintain a consistent vigilant effort. The effort is not to be considered a luxury but an essential ingredient for mission-based marketing in the twenty-first century. Yet the present reality indicates that churches are woefully unprepared to effectively carry out the tasks in cyberspace.

The Soul of Cyberspace

Does cyberspace have a soul? Well, it is an intriguing concept; however, as we study cyberculture with the lenses of faith, religion, or spirituality we observe a growing reality of traditional and nontraditional religious groups positioning themselves in cyberspace. In his book *The Soul of Cyberspace,* Jeff Zaleski stirred up a lot of interest by his comprehensive focus on the expanding religious reality.[13] His book is one of the navigational tools that aids in coming to initial terms and perspectives with the new religious phenomenon in cyberspace. Moslems, Jews, Buddhists, Hindus, Catholics and other Christians, and many New Age religious groups have claimed territory in cyberspace. Yet, it is not only a matter of claiming territory—or space. It is the actual dynamics of interpersonal relationship and formation of new virtual communities that sparks our ongoing interest.

Consider for a moment the idea of religious rituals in cyberspace. Is it possible to hold rituals here? The answer is yes, and it is happening as you read these pages. While some segments of the Church continue to query the orthopraxis of televising Mass, cyberspace is expanding the reality. It may be possible that some elements of traditional ritual may be lost without physical presence. Yet, what happens when participants gather synchronously on a regular basis for cyber rituals, cyber prayer meetings, or cyber paraliturgies? Can we say it is not an authentic religious experience or prayer?

McLuhan said every new technology changes the way our sense organs operate to perceive reality, and it may be that computer technology and the Internet change not only our perception of reality and the ministry of the Church but also our very selves. The extent of demand for greater and greater interdependency in Internet interaction compels us to consider it more than just an instrument or a machine. It shares our social lives and thus engages in psychological development.[14] It has forced us to rethink technology as practice instead of mere technique. The holding power of computing can create a twilight zone of electronic time and space and lived time. It is seen as an authentic extension of our being. It is rapidly becoming our consciousness and nervous system.

The new profession of Webmaster has nurtured new mindsets about how to design, position, and attract visitors or cyberzens to one's Web site. Web sites are more than locations for "hunting and gathering" information. They are sites for interactivity. Synchronous and asynchronous Web sites supported with e-mail, discussion boards, chatrooms, and live video conversations and classes are capturing the imagination of cyber explorers and spiritual seekers. Cyberspace is a serious place for serious seekers. How the Church images and positions herself within this space is very important. Those who navigate through cyberspace on a regular basis have come to expect imagination, attractiveness, interactivity, and the unfolding of fresh or new information. Thus we find the sites most frequently visited are those that are presented in a creative, inspiring, and interactive way. It is by way of such sites that we discover the formation of spiritual and faith communities consisting of people who make covenants with one another. They regularly present themselves in cyberspace within their chat. These experiences are further supported by ongoing opportunities in religious and spiritual education courses, workshops, and seminars.

Cyberspace is a democratic zone. Rob Shields states that the principal paradigm of the Net is not control but dissemination. Not "them against us," not the zero-sum scenario as in the old mass media models, but rather the win-win technology of the Web.[15] In relation to religion and spirituality, for example, one can explore, find, and compare theologies and religious thought through the simple support of any Internet search engine. These engines have a vast reach and can swiftly bring one to the door of any church or religious association. Within cyberspace, however, the Church cannot control the explorations and experiences of her members or interested "cyberzens." This is a scary reality for those who perceive that control is essential. As we have seen in earlier chapters, the vast new religious panorama that employs intriguing marketing techniques—especially in cyberspace—demands that the Church prepare her ministers for research, design, and active participation in that arena. It is here that a new evangelization is blossoming forth based on a new language, new psychology, and new techniques.

—) Conclusion

We are living in a time between parentheses. The future is quickly closing in upon us. We have seen that the religious panorama within which we live is diverse, complex, and vast and rapidly changing. What initiatives are being designed to guide forward the Church's evangelization and catechetical efforts in the media, and particularly cyberspace? The downside of answering this question appears to be that no sooner do we attempt to respond with a specific description than a new reality has been conceived and positioned. Cyberspace is vast and deep. Even with the high-powered search engines we cannot decipher precisely what is happening in cyberspace. The best metaphor to apply to one's research in cyberspace is an archeological dig. One must be persistent, patient, and profoundly investigative to explore the realms of cyberspace.

Specific criteria must be applied when considering utilizing the new media or the Internet for our ministry endeavors:

- Does it enhance the quality of our conversations?

- Does it evoke a greater sense of collaboration, thus initiating new paradigms of faith communities?

- Does it stimulate critical reflection and discernment?

- Does it encourage creativity, adaptation, and apperception?

- Does it stimulate conversion or transformation toward new methodologies for facilitating learning and proclamation of the Gospel?

- Does it motivate commitment both to a deeper understanding of our covenant of faith and to study and research of new styles of communicating?

- Does it encourage and support a contemplative presence?

We need to consider ourselves as artists of faith in the mediasphere. We have new tools that offer us creative opportunities to pioneer within the new frontier. This is not a time for lone rangers, but for collaborators and innovators. Our quest is to break out of our traditional paradigms and navigate into new learning environments.

We can stimulate the religious imagination of the peoples of the world through creative application of the media and the Internet and by motivating people to enter into a dynamic dialogue of faith not only among their local faith community but the world. Thus, we come to understand that *Catholic* truly means universal.

In her book *Life on the Screen,* Sherry Turkle says that opportunities are being created to build new kinds of communities, virtual communities in which we participate with people from all over the world, people with whom we converse daily, people with whom we may have fairly intimate relationships although we may never physically meet.[16] Thus, the perception of what we traditionally have understood by Christian communities or faith communities is undergoing a paradigm shift in cyberspace. Not only are the type and format of our stories shifting, so also are the place and location where stories are communicated and reformulated for a new generation of believers.

—) **Q**uestions for Reflection

1. Identify areas in your faith life where there has been significant change. Identify areas in your parish life where there has been significant change. How did you respond to the change? What did you learn?

2. What are some new approaches or techniques that might be used to image and echo God in the world, within our families, friends, and neighborhoods?

3. How might your parish (the Church) engage the Internet as a valuable means for evangelization and faith formation? How can clerics and lay ecclesial ministers best acquire the skill in the application of computers and the Internet for ministry?

4. What have you found most helpful for your personal religious life as you navigate in cyberspace?

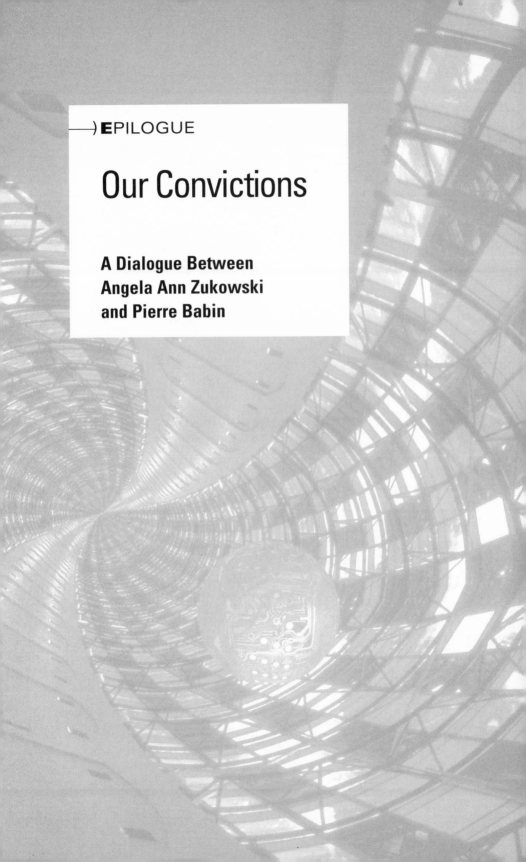

Our Convictions

**A Dialogue Between
Angela Ann Zukowski
and Pierre Babin**

Writing the last lines of their book, in the course of a kind of "summit meeting," the two authors engage in a reflection on the fundamental themes they are developing in their ministries. They are interviewed by Ferdinand Poswick, a Benedictine Brother of Maredsous (Belgium) well known for his studies on Bible and computer science.

FERDINAND **P**OSWICK **Writing your book, did you perceive a certain evolution in your thinking? What are your main points?**

ANGELA **A**NN **Z**UKOWSKI I see three key points that are relevant to our conversation.

First, we are living in the midst of a new culture. This is articulated not only within Vatican documents like *Redemptoris Missio* and *Aetatis Novae* but by observing what is going on around us. This new culture is the media or what I call the Infomedia culture. I call it Infomedia because it is the convergence of information and diverse media into new patterns of communications. Thus, this new culture manifests itself with evolving creeds, codes, and cults (rituals). As Catholic communicators, we must be able to understand, interpret, and engage this culture for our ministries in the twenty-first century.

I believe that our understanding of a new evangelization requires a deep appreciation for this culture. This new Infomedia culture has many dimensions. It is not only a single technique or technology. It is many media or communication technologies in concert.

Therefore, I like to use the image of a kaleidoscope to describe this New Age. A kaleidoscope has many diverse pieces that constitute each design. As we turn the kaleidoscope, our eyes capture a new perspective and a new relationship of the pieces to one another. This awakens an "aha" experience. There is more than one way to see. As we shift our focus, or perspective, a new way of seeing the pieces in relationship to one another emerges before us. The same thing happens when we consider the new evangelization within the new Infomedia culture. Each new medium offers a new approach, a different design or impact to enhance our evangelization efforts.

This is the challenge that we have before us as we engage in the call for a new evangelization. The new evangelization calls for a new kaleidoscopic approach to ministry. We need to keep asking ourselves a basic question: What is the most effective way we can use the infomedia to evangelize in the twenty-first century? We must be inclusive rather than exclusive in our infomedia approach to evangelization.

Second, the new evangelization calls for a radical paradigm shift. The world has changed dramatically in the past twenty-five years. All indicators suggest that the speed of change will continue to accelerate offering us a new world order. We are discovering that there is a new way of seeing, knowing, living (acting), and "being" within the world that is different. We realize we cannot function out of the same paradigm as in years gone by. The complexity and interrelationships of life in the world call for new patterns (paradigms) for understanding the world and our relationship to the world and one another. This leads to a fundamental question: what impact do these new patterns have on our evangelization efforts?

Third, the new reality of cyberspace for evangelization must be acknowledged as an important reality. The Internet (World Wide Web) offers us a new place to evangelize. As more and more people are spending more and more time in cyberspace, it is formally becoming recognized as a "new place." This new place is a "virtual place" but it is still a place where people meet and engage in conversation and community. It must be taken seriously as we both engage in the formation of evangelizers and evangelize.

PIERRE **B**ABIN   At first, I was writing this book with a very personal approach, but, as the work proceeded, I experienced new developments. I used to think that the young, and also the population in general, were not so open to evangelization.

- On the one hand, a new way of talking—that of television and journalism—prevails. I used to see that language as a chance for faith to grow.

- On another hand, traditional evangelization, formal preaching and catechesis, seemed to me not at all appropriate for communication in that new language. Instead of communicating religious leaders were more often reacting against the new languages.

In light of that perception, I believe that the two most important points of the integration of culture in evangelization would be seeing evangelization as *commerce,* and the message as *body.*

It is very difficult to accept the word *commerce* when we link it to evangelization. I faced resistance from some people; from others I have received encouragement. At the last CREC-AVEX Congress in Lyon, a participant—a Protestant—told me: "Please, do not use the word *dialogue,* that will drown the fish we are trying to catch. Go on with *commerce* and say that the new communication model is *commerce;* that is to say an exchange of goods after bargaining." I think that we must eliminate the manner of giving without receiving, of preaching without "feedback," without an "exchange." Except in some particular situations, communication should happen in the right way, as a *commercial* conversation, as a compromise.

The second important point concerns the message as "body"; the message is not doctrine, it is "my body." It is who I am, what I can express, according to the environment and the technologies I am linked to. I caught sight of this when I realized that the audiovisual language is in essence just like "modulation," a trait of electronically amplified vibrations. If this is so, when we use the audiovisual language to establish a conversation, we transmit vibrations. Thus it seemed to me that this is an extraordinary chance for the non-occidental cultures, Latin America, Asia, and Africa. For all the "poor," generally speaking, who do not have access to the intellectual language and who comprehend through rock, rap, and sports. In a word, there is a chance for all who express themselves as "modulators."

Another important point: Both Angela Ann and I like this era; we like the electronic technologies. We are seeing their possibilities before us as well as their risks. So, I just wanted a book of "inspiration," dynamic, a positive contribution to face the media culture and the people who are immersed on it.

FERDINAND **P**OSWICK **Do you think that these key points are appealing to young people inside the Church to change their mind? Do you think that the key points the two of you have made are really appealing to the people who are living today and are searching for something? Have you met with people who have need of those kinds of paradigms?**

ANGELA **A**NN **Z**UKOWSKI There is no question in my mind that the young people especially are coming out of the situation that we address in our book. Young people today know in a multimedia fashion. What comes to mind is the work of Howard Gardner. In his book *Frames of Mind: Multiple Intelligences* he speaks about the many ways of knowing—for both teaching and learning. He indicates that there are varying types and degrees of giftedness and intelligence in people and we should appeal to them all for effective communication. The seven are: (1) linguistic, (2) musical, (3) logical, (4) spatial, (5) kinesthetic, (6) interpersonal, and (7) intrapersonal. I think Gardner's research relates perfectly well to the youth of today. The new Infomedia culture engages most if not all of these intelligences in one way or another. Thus, we in ministry cannot ignore either the form or the process for effective evangelization.

We see that young people today learn through all the senses in multiple diverse ways. I think there is a relationship here to what Pierre means when he speaks about the stereo effect within our life experiences. Young people today are learning in and through a multimedia approach. All their senses are engaged in capturing the world around them. I can document this in two ways. First, I am very much aware that in my undergraduate classes my students need both the audio and the visual to learn. If I want to hold their attention and be assured that the information being shared is communicated and has taken hold, I must speak but I must accompany my theological concepts with visuals. The simultaneous communication of audio and visual is imperative to my students' understanding. Lecture alone does not work. The young people of the twenty-first century are no longer conditioned to these "mono" methodologies.

I can also call upon the experiences that are taking place in Catholic elementary schools in my country. Young people are using computers as part of their basic learning experiences. They are required at an early age (seven to nine years) to produce multimedia projects. Students collect their multimedia projects over their elementary years. They are saved on a diskette and are referred to as multimedia portfolios. These become one of the measures of achievement and excellence in learning. So, as I visit Catholic schools I see that students do not limit themselves to pen and paper or words alone to communicate ideas. The youth today use images, sound, music, and text together to communicate their ideas and new understandings. Their frame of reference for communicating emerges out of the new Infomedia culture.

Second, young people today are more interactive rather than passive in their learning. As I indicated before, lecture alone does not work. We need to engage conversation or dialogue in an interactive learning environment in order to stimulate the religious imagination. The religious imagination today does not move an individual by means of a passive methodology, that is, by simply hearing or reading a fact or idea. It requires interactivity. It is stimulated when people come together. No matter how they come together—in physical or virtual space—they do come together to exchange meaning, ideas, and direction. This is where young people are today. This new paradigm calls for a new kaleidoscopic ministry.

I venture to say that as more and more people (youth, adults, and older adults) become familiar and at home with the new Infomedia culture their learning will be enriched, challenged, and animated. As I indicated, the new Infomedia culture engages all the senses. I find that when all the senses are engaged, one's experience of spirituality is deepened as well. Once this happens individuals are able to articulate their faith experience in more concrete ways than they had in the past. I feel that faith experience in the past was either superficial or intuitive. It was superficial in so far as the initial introduction to the faith was not an existential fit. There was not a relationship between the individuals' actual experience of the Gospel or All Holy and what was being communicated about the faith. Thus, individuals accepted the abstract reality because of the pressure of the context or the socialization demanded by the environment. This does not mean that an authentic faith experience could not occur. It only means that the personal experience was often difficult to articulate within the abstract or unfamiliar context.

The intuitive communication of faith is a valid form of communication. This is expressed and experienced in and through the life of the family or faith community. In this context faith is woven into the fabric of life. People's lives within the faith community become a narrative of faith stories communicating the culture and meaning of faith. This is essential for weaving the Good News into the nurturing process of the individual. It is essential for the ongoing formation and direction of lived faith. In this sense faith can be identified as intuitive faith. The faith narrative becomes the individual's personal story. Yet, for conversion and commitment to occur the personal experience of faith needs to be expressed and communicated in images, words, symbols, and sounds reflective of or associated with the personal experience.

Today I think this new Infomedia culture gives women, men, and children additional tools or techniques needed to express what they feel and think about their religious experiences. Experience (the personal encounter with Jesus or the All Holy); faith (saying "yes" to the experience); and theology (naming the experience and the "yes") form a concentric circle. It is a never-ending circle inviting the individual to a richer and deeper understanding, expression, and commitment of faith to the Gospel. It is dynamic. It is never ending. Thus, at each phase or stage of our life we seek out new means of expression and communication. The new Infomedia culture offers us another means to engage in communicating the Good News.

PIERRE BABIN I am not going to say a lot about the youth, except to point out the Taizé experience and the World Youth Day in Paris in 1997 with Pope John Paul II. I saw those enthusiastic young people and how they were deeply influenced, how some of them became converted. This book is trying to explain the new reality as a new way of experiencing the Christian life.

I know in our countries many communicators, catechists, and priests working in the field of religious communication are quite desperately concerned. They do not see the new culture as an opportunity. They see all these new technologies only as occasions of entertainment or useful tools. Finally, they are tempted to think that communication must be used primarily to deliver doctrine. Media? A "little bit of sugar" to give doctrine a good taste! Unconsciously confined in that pattern, they consign technologies to the accessories storehouse.

I hope our book will help our readers to understand that it is not simply a matter of amplifying a doctrinal speech with the media; the challenge is to deeply transform the communication system. The time is coming to put an end to a pessimistic attitude. Many people have told us: "We feel so alone. Our ecclesiastical leaders don't help us. If we try to test the new language of the young people, we have to face the burden of the institutions."

FERDINAND **P**OSWICK **Does this reflection and conversation of many years change something in yourself and in the way you are communicating?**

ANGELA **A**NN **Z**UKOWSKI I think I can answer the question from two perspectives. First, I believe something unique was stimulated between Pierre and myself through our conversations; and, second, there is an ongoing evaluation in my own new appreciation and understanding of the new Infomedia culture.

First, when Pierre and I began our conversation several years ago we were in two different places. We had our own paradigms from which we were engaging in our theological reflections, conversations, and ministry. This is understandable since he is French and I am American; he a man and I a woman; our education, life experiences, media expertise and perspectives, and international focus differed in whole or part. Our encounters and conversations over the years have enabled us to let go of some of our ideas and really listen to the other person's experiences and perspectives.

I believe we have come to an appreciation of our diversity—
or perhaps our unity in our diversity. We have really enjoyed seeing how our paradigms may differ, how each one's paradigm
teases the other's out in richer detail. In one sense we have come
to see how twisting or turning the kaleidoscope brings forth an
alternative valued frame of reference. I have been teased to
rethink my paradigm especially as I observe how others respond
to Pierre's insights into his paradigm. All this makes our conversations quite exciting as we see new possibilities for evangelization and catechesis emerge.

Second, we have spent much time reflecting on the word
evangelization. We have come to realize that the term carries a
lot of historical baggage with it. It is difficult to move away from
it no matter how you look at the term or the language of evangelization. We firmly agree that evangelization is not proselytiza-
tion. Evangelization is more than conversion. Evangelization is
coming to mean a way of being present in our families, parish,
community, and world. It is first and foremost fundamentally a
way of being—a way of living the Gospel through our ordinary
lives. It is associated with what it means to be human with a
Christian lens. Was not this the message of St. Paul?

If we really want to evangelize in the new marketplace of the
Infomedia culture, we have to come to the marketplace with a
new name or understanding of the means of evangelization. We
already know from reading the documents from the five Synods
that prepared for the Jubilee year that all of them are seeking a
new means related to their cultural context. Thus, we need to
keep turning the kaleidoscope for a new perspective.

PIERRE **B**ABIN Our dialogue—I prefer to say conversation/conver-
sion—took place on a three-point level:

1. At first, "the prophetic imagination"; it is one of Angela Ann's
key words. My own key word was "modulation." Then, working with Angela Ann, I brought the two terms together. The
language of modulation develops imagination and forces us to
think again of faith in an imaginary and a prophetic way. I
think that we have to reformulate with imagination the old cat-

echetical notions that are locked up in venerable texts. We have to keep these but re-create them. We have to rethink our faith again, with our young people's groups, according to *their* imagination and *their* emotion, with music and image. For example, I used to listen with groups to Pierre Henry's music "Le livre des morts egyptiens" and to ask them: What images and colors do you see when listening to the music? How do you imagine death and resurrection, the body and the soul? What link do you see between your images, your ideas and the Church's?

2. The second element I found helpful in working with Angela Ann is her mediatic style of holding a conference. When she speaks to a group of people, she is always making abundant use of projectors, screens, videos, and electronic tools: a full bag! That is effectively a mediatic communication. So, I realized that I was too dependent on the written text. My body was an audiovisual, but the tools I was using were not. Little by little, I am rectifying my manner of teaching, thanks to an extending of my body through electronic media.

3. Finally, the communication summit is not the conference, but the dialogue. Indeed, we need lectures and sermons, but first of all let us have a dialogue allowing each one to play an active role. A great twentieth-century religious person, Madeleine Delbrel, who was living in the heart of a Paris suburb, said: "To evangelize is not to converse. Only two words express the summit of evangelization: presence and dialogue." Today, I do not see any other way to communicate faith in the Global Village. Dialogue, Internet, worldwide and interrelegious *commerce,* these are the new ways to be discovered.

FERDINAND **P**OSWICK **Media, a change more than a risk? Do you have any wishes to express?**

ANGELA **A**NN **Z**UKOWSKI I was giving a parish retreat last year. The parish council was gathered to discern how they might discover new ways for stimulating a new evangelization effort both within and outside the faith community. During the retreat the parishioners came to realize that it was not a program they needed. It fundamentally was not a new activity, but there was something much deeper at the heart of the idea of evangelization that began to glow. They realized the parish needed to be rooted in a clearer understanding and lived reality of a theology of presence, a theology of environment, and a theology of conversation or dialogue. This meant they needed to spend time thinking about

1. the quality of the parishioners lives (presence) among one another (the faith community) and outside (local culture),

2. the quality of both the welcoming and spatial environment of the parish and finally,

3. the quality of the richness, depth, and diversity of their conversations/dialogues with people of all generations regarding their personal experiences of Jesus—the Good News.

They realized that if these conditions were not in place, all the evangelization activities or programs could be meaningless and ineffective.

I believe a new term is needed to bring those three ideas into play as fundamental. I believe in new words. New words energize and refocus our creativity, ideas, and plans of action. New words are dynamic. New words, like new ideas, free us of old baggage and lighten the load—opening us to the working of the Holy Spirit in the new marketplace of the new millennium.

FERDINAND **P**OSWICK **What are your hopes for future development? Are you optimistic?**

ANGELA **A**NN **Z**UKOWSKI I have two basic hopes as outcomes of our work. First, that our readers come to realize that the new info-media that are at our service today are an important and valuable means of artistic expression for the Good News. These techniques or tools can help to stimulate the religious imagination in order to proclaim the Good News. Art has always played an important role in the history of the Church. These new media are the modern techniques of art for the new marketplace—the new culture. If our readers can be inspired to think of the new info-media as new art forms for expressing and experiencing the

Good News, their paradigm may begin to shift. They can begin to experience a new freedom or release of creativity

If parish leaders, catechists, and evangelizers begin to think of themselves as artisans or artists of faith in contemporary culture, the infomedia can become their new tools or techniques for the religious imagination and for new great conversations concerning faith in our world.

Second, that our focus is not on getting numbers but on nurturing an environment that stimulates a passion for the Good News. We begin to think outside the box and ask what alternative approaches are available to us. It is not the tyranny of either/or, it is both/and. There are many ways open to us to evangelize and we must employ them all. Ultimately we must understand these are only techniques to be engaged for reaching a lived reality of the Gospel within the lives of women and men today.

PIERRE BABIN For my part, it's most important to be optimistic. This is based on my faith in God, in life, in the human person! Among young people and many other persons, I feel an expectation, a great spiritual desire, I see astonishing realizations, a springtime blossoming! May our readers distinguish the Spirit who is moving ahead of us.

Then, what I would wish? Well! I believe that many of our contemporary people are acting just like the sick persons around the Bethesda swimming pool; they are waiting for the water to move. They are waiting for a modulation generated by the Church for a connection with their expectations.

I wish to create high "spiritual modulation" circles, prayer and creation communities, with people who are media, people who are symbols. I think that the audience is waiting for individuals or mediating groups full of God's vitality.

In spite of the origin of the word, I radically refuse to reduce the media to simple methodologies. People are always asking me: what means should we use? I tell them: "That is not the problem! You do not 'use' the media, you are yourselves the *medium*. If you act as medium, you will use the media; but above all, you will become yourself the medium, become a body who has something to say, who lives a full life, who is free. Be imaginative and, automatically, you will become yourself the Internet, video, sound, and the like. The audience is waiting for you as medium, in the full sense of the word: a mediator."

Another of my wishes concerns the Church. As we are beginning the twenty-first century I should like to see that the Church take a step forward and recognize the world of pluralism. I do not see how we can enter this new century if we do not integrate pluralism into the Church's pastoral consciousness. Recently, I was talking with the director of a Pastoral Institute. He told me that the main future concern of the theologians will be to determine how the Church will integrate pluralism. I agree.

FERDINAND **P**OSWICK **If you had really to advise Church leaders, what would be the two or three points you would stress?**

PIERRE **B**ABIN As it was often said in the Unda/OCIC Congresses, the first priority is unquestionably formation.

1. It is of cardinal importance for the Church's leaders—the bishops and the national directors of services—to have a clear sense of the new culture. At all costs, they must move away from the idea that media must be used as a "vehicle to disseminate the doctrine" to the idea that media is in itself culture and language. Imagine Italians arriving in New York doing their best to speak English over three, four, or five years in order to survive, in an Italian way, in New York; quite so! No problem. But eventually, when you are living in a country that has its own language and its specific culture, you have to speak that language and to acquire the "American way of life." Well, I think the time is coming to stop considering audiovisual as a way to survive and trying to maintain an old system; it is a new culture. The immersion of the bishops in the media culture is a priority for conscience' sake, in order to open the Gospel to everyone.

2. Second, seminaries remain high places for the Gutenberg print culture. That culture is a necessary one with a priority in matter of formation. But, aside from the traditional culture, we

should promote another type of formation. A different formation with its own contents and methods, giving wide place to
modulation and emotion, where the economy of exchange is
essential, where the Global Village is integrated to the local
one. We have to insist: it is not a question of ability to handle
technology, but to assume the culture linked to technology, in
short, to learn the "media way of life." And, surely, that is
impossible without technology.

3. Finally, I think that we have to train a certain number of people who will be able to take over the information in seminaries, in religious communities, in regions, in short, to work on a
ground level without being experts or "pros." These people
should know well the mediatic culture and how it is functioning. They should be able to master and to use the basic technologies (sound, camera, editing, computer, etc.): the principles of language are the same in all the electronic technologies.

ANGELA **A**NN **Z**UKOWSKI In our first chapter we discussed the shifting pastoral, cross-cultural, and media situations that are occur-
ring throughout the world today. Church leaders need to take
these changes to heart and realize there is a connection between
them. They do not stand in isolation. Thus, it is imperative that
we rethink our paradigm of what it means to be Church today.
We are challenged to find new ways of being Church.

Second, all our formation programs for Church leadership, in
catechesis, evangelization, and pastoral ministry must contain a
strong foundation in understanding and application of the new
Infomedia culture to our ways of being Church. If we do not ensure
that our seminaries, religious houses of formation and ministry formation, and catechetical training centers introduce new skills related to this new culture we are in for real trouble. The Church will
continue doing what she has been doing for the past hundred
years. As Einstein said, "Absolute madness is doing the same thing
over and over and over again and expecting different results." I feel
this is what we frequently do within the Church. We do not shift
our techniques for communicating the Gospel. We continue to use
the same homilies, parish activities, and evangelization techniques.
It is like putting new wine into old wineskins. If the Gospel is not

caught, we blame the people instead of rethinking our traditional process of communication for transformation.

If we are concerned about the future of the Church, let's talk with the people who are the future. This means let's engage the youth in a great exploration for packaging the Good News within the new marketplace of the world. We must do this now and not tomorrow.

Third, I indicated earlier that art is important. We must have a renaissance of religious artists and art within the church. If we are to evangelize effectively, we need to encourage artists to blossom within the Church. A ministry of artists must be as fundamental as any other ministry within the Church. Our youth must find an outlet for artistic religious expression within the Church. The new Infomedia culture calls for artistic skills. These are needed in order to engage in mission-based marketing—for positioning, imaging, and stimulating the religious imagination today. Our expression of faith cannot be limited to theological abstract thinking; it must include artistic religious imagination as well. Therefore, the Church must support art. I even think that dioceses should have some form of artists in residence, or Diocesan Fellows, who assume a sabbatical year to assist the Church in religious expression through the new Infomedia culture.

FERDINAND **P**OSWICK **Are we going to put formation for media in a privileged position? Are we going to give it a priority on all the other types of formation?**

ANGELA **A**NN **Z**UKOWSKI I don't think it is an either/or situation. I go back to what I said earlier about the tyranny of either/or before. The tyranny of either/or is again playing out here. Church formation tends to be compartmentalized. We need to rethink our curriculum in formation. How we teach theology and philosophy is just as important as their content. The methodology carries a message on how to communicate within the Church. If we desire a new form of communication for a new evangelization, it must be modeled into the formation programs themselves. So, our professors in these formation programs also need formation in communication processes and skills. The academic community is the most difficult culture to shift. I know. I am part of an academic community.

I do think there are specific communication and infomedia courses that need to be taught as part of the base curriculum in formation programs. I also firmly believe that the application of communication techniques and skills needs to be woven into the fabric of the learning experience rather than treated as a separate subject. The kaleidoscopic perspective I spoke about earlier needs to be applied here. The young people who are entering our seminaries and formation houses are very creative women and men. We need to build on their creativity. We see that many of them are already coming to us with great media knowledge and skills and a way of life from their concrete everyday experience of the Infomedia culture. The problems and concerns that the professors in the late 1990s and early 2000s have with the new Infomedia culture will be short lived with the new candidates in our midst. So, let's not go backward in our formation and training but forward! Yes, let us rethink our curriculum and reflect a positive proactive dynamic for teaching and learning that are emerging via the Infomedia culture.

PIERRE **B**ABIN I differ a little bit with Angela Ann. That obliges me to say how I see this problem. Surely, it is not a question of replacing the basic formation in seminaries with training in media or in communication. No, the study of philosophy and other studies that provide a rigorous, scientific, and rational foundation for future religious leaders is indispensable. How can we form leaders today without a scientific culture, without a rational approach, without an apprenticeship of clear and precise language?

In addition we have to organize other formation programs. When I say "in addition," I am not saying that the seminary should fix a two-hour weekly communication course. I do not believe in it. This is not the question. We cannot produce a radio or television scenario in two hours in a lecture room. We need a longer period, at another site, making use of another formation system. We need immersion in today's culture. And that requires at least a week here, or a week there. Or maybe a three-or six-month session—I do not know. But I would insist upon keeping the two types of formation, using the analogy of the two-sided brain function: left brain and right brain. I would say that the traditional school trains the left brain. Good. Indispensable. But now, let us also train the right brain. It is true that we need an integrated formation system, but how can we expect to realize integration without first admitting the existence of two original cultures, of both an intellectual and an affective approach? In France, we have art schools and letters universities, two sites and two systems. If, as Angela said, the new technologies are rather on the art side, then, it is important for seminary programs to make sure there is a certain distance and difference between the two apprenticeships: the art one and the Gutenberg one.

ANGELA ANN ZUKOWSKI That question of formation is definitely very important. We often say, "that you will teach the same way you have been trained yourself." I also think that the way we are going to practice ministry will reflect our training style. We have a cohesive global "system," and if something must change, it is the whole system that should be toppled. In our situation, that seems to be the most important thing, but also the most difficult, because within the Church, it is difficult to change the whole system. However, I believe that in our formation programs the right target is systemic change. I am convinced that this process, which is conducting someone to assume a significant function of responsibility or ministry in the Church, requires a formation program that is the very model of ministry or responsibility the individual will have to pursue tomorrow.

But nothing is going to move if we don't have the courage to change the whole system. As soon as we talk systemic change, we take fright. This is what we are saying in this book. This does not necessarily mean that we are losing everything. But it means that all the pedagogic experiences we have been concerned about, fought for, and once considered to be immutable are marked out for change!

Maybe we should express our wishes, our ideas in the form of a question to be urgently directed to those who are responsible for the formation in the Church: what kind of formation or what educative process is today indispensable to spread the Gospel in the heart of that new media culture? In our context, what new formula should be utilized to enhance, to support the catechists, the ministers, the persons responsible in the Church, in order to proclaim the Gospel effectively and efficaciously in the twenty-first century? This is the question!

PIERRE BABIN I am thinking of what Angela Ann said. It is urgent. It calls for a deep change in the system. The Council of Trent also changed the system after the invention of the printing press.

FERDINAND POSWICK **Does your dialogue, your research, bring you to see Jesus differently?**

ANGELA ANN ZUKOWSKI The dynamic that is emerging from our approach is that at the time of a new media culture, "experience" is more important than ever for our spiritual growth. And when we say "experience" we are saying that all our senses are in contact with the Almighty, with the Transcendent. By using all our senses, our religious imagination is stimulated. The religious reality becomes "bone of our bones and flesh of our flesh"! It is not an accessory that we put on only on Sunday; it is incorporated into our own person, it becomes our breath.

Writing this book, through this conversation, I was (and I am still) in quest of new ways to have an experience of Jesus. I am trying unceasingly to pursue the question What can I do to stimulate a religious personal response in others?

It is not a question of fixing our eyes on certain transcendence, somewhere, over there, beyond us! No! It is a call to live consciously the Incarnation. Here is the Word! The symbol I consider as a more and more significant one, for our consumption in this book, is Rublev's Trinity icon. This icon is a door to a greater understanding of authentic communication and community within our ministries and parish life today.

PIERRE BABIN Am I getting on in years? Is it the media culture? I went through two periods.

In the first one I was young, asking myself: is it really Jesus who fulfills what it means to be a human being?

There was a time when I dropped everything, because I did not think that Church, with its catechism, its dogma, and its morality, was answering my question. The world—at least the one I was seeing—seemed to be more in accord with my life. Then, all of a sudden change occurred—was it faith? I was surprised; I believed that He was really Himself, Jesus, the Good News. You see, the word came. I said: "I will live a good life, I am ready to be faithful, but on condition that it is a Good News for every human being. If Hell or if any truth we are teaching is not the Good News, I leave now, I will go away."

It is difficult to talk about the second period. It could be what Augustine described as Jesus "closer to myself than myself." Jesus bonded with people whose lives were devoid of meaning, who were morally tired and terribly lonely. There are so many religions, so many doctrines, so many encounters, so many stars in the world, a world shaken up by the media. How can we withstand the experience of being moved by such a multiplicity of emotions and turbulences? How can we be happy, at peace, without being "tied down" to the heavy armor of the Church's teaching and moral demands? Finally, isn't everything relative? And is the Catholic Church just one among others, nothing more? Do we ask God for help, or call upon Jesus? It is just like speaking into a washing machine; we only hear in return the echo of our own voice.

How do we answer such questions? I was facing an indescribable transformation. I had perceived a gift. I was conscious of a *thin* voice coinciding with an interior emptiness and saying: I Am (and when I say I Am, I am Yahweh!). Such was the answer beyond the question. The old image of an external God that I used to see became a more intimate image. "I *Am*" was from myself, higher than me, deeply in my interior and in my liberty: the echo of my voice had taken on a transcendental sound! That experience marked the starting point of another perception of Jesus. I was discerning my own mystery and I grafted Jesus onto this mystery that is myself. In the thin voice awake in the depths of myself, I perceived a fragile Christ (a sound of sheer silence . . . said Elijah) and at the same time totally certain, permanent (my deep ego being unchanged). I meditate day after day, mixing my inner voice with the Jesus of the Gospel.

I am not saying that I see this Christ in others, as we see a photograph. No, and besides the word "see" is too strong a word: let us rather say that I find Christ thanks to an interior connection. I find him in the other, in the friend, in the stranger, in so far as he is "Totally Other" (en français: "Tout-Autre"), in other words, an aspect of myself not yet awakened, but also a fascinating and impossible Horizon. Moreover, in the interior of my relationship with the other, I abandon my own being, my images, and my dogmatic conceptions. In the name of my concern for the other, I make an experiment of Jesus as Medium, not fixed as a standing statue, but as "In Between," as Love.

I am deeply comfortable with this maxim of Mencius, a sixth-century Chinese sage: "The man of a different race is a forgotten aspect of ourselves, and, thus he is a secret mirror of God." If I can say, with the interreligious dialogue ("commerce" in its full sense), I enter into my own totality and, at the same time, into this act itself, I better discern the Christ of the Gospel. From another point of view, being medium, I become Christ-Love to some small extent.

Evidently, that knowledge of Christ turns into an endless quest. It does not transform me into in a pillar of the Church, but rather into a pilgrim: in that sense, I feel like a brother of the unbelievers and also of the many young people who have misgivings about life. At the same time a certainty and a force dwell in me that other people sometimes tell me about; force and certainty that are perhaps more perceptible as I am no more in possession of them. A paradox . . .

I think that Jesus (the one I am now referring to) corresponds better with the spirit of time, because he is emerging less from an exterior education than from the profound depths of my inner being. This is an experience of identity and sensibility that the knowledge of Jesus gives to the body.

FERDINAND **P**OSWICK **How do you see young people and the future?**

PIERRE **B**ABIN I finish by recalling Taizé, not only as a reality, but also as an image of the future . . . Jesus? Thousands and thousands of young people sitting or lying on the floor, in the church. The shining light of many candles, the glints of light through the stained glass window, the choirs, the music, and this child voice singing: "there is no greater love than to give our life for those we love."

If the surrounding atmosphere is supportive, young people are able to experience silence. Thus, they are able to listen to the inner voice speaking from the bottom of their heart where Jesus is talking. They are ready to give their life for those they love.

Notes

CHAPTER 1

1. *Time,* 5 April 1993.
2. *U.S. News and World Report,* 29 March 1993.
3. *Newsweek,* 10 April 1995.
4. *U.S. News and World Report,* 13 March 1995.
5. *U.S. News and World Report,* 17 April 1995.
6. *U.S. News and World Report,* 9 September 1996.
7. *Time,* 23 October 1996.
8. Ibid.
9. *Maclean's,* 15 December 1995.
10. *Life,* December 1998.
11. Thomas Fox, *Catholicism on the Web* (Holt, 1997).
12. *Time,* 23 December 1996.
13. Jeff Zaleski, *The Soul of Cyberspace* (HarperSanFrancisco, 1997).
14. *Time,* 23 December 1996, 62.
15. William Bausch, *Pilgrim Church* (Twenty-Third Publications, 1989), 431.
16. Philip Gleason, ed., *Catholicism in America* (Harper & Row, 1970), 150.
17. Richard Cimino and Don Lattin, *Shopping for Faith* (Jossey-Bass, 1998).
18. Schneiders states that "Postmodernity is both a child of and a protest against modernity, which is itself a child of the Enlightenment." She indicates three features of Postmodernity: (1) a loss of unitary worldview and the resulting fragmentation of reality on every level; (2) subversion of foundations—there is nothing stable on which to base one's thoughts; and (3) the subversion of metanarratives. She defines *metanarrative* as a master story that one believes comprehends the whole of reality and into which one's own story fits. Sandra Schneiders, *Finding the Treasure* (Paulist Press, 2000), 111 ff.
19. William Bausch, *The Parish of the Next Millennium* (Twenty-Third Publications, 1997).
20. Robert White, unpublished paper entitled "Communication and Evangelization in Europe," 1988.
21. James Bacik, *The Gracious Mystery: Finding God in Ordinary Experience* (St. Anthony Messenger, 1987).
22. *Commonweal,* 15 September 1998.
23. Robert Ludwig, *Reconstructing Catholicism* (Crossroad 1995), 139.
24. Richard Cimino and Don Lattin, op. cit.
25. Ibid., 38.
26. Ibid., 39.
27. Robert Wuthnow, *Christianity in the Twenty-First Century* (Oxford University Press, 1993), 120.
28. David Tracy, *On Naming the Present* (Orbis, 1994), 11.

29. Edgar A. Towne, "Fundamentalism's Theological Challenge to the Churches," in *Fundamentalism Today,* ed. Marla Selvidge (Brethren Press, 1984).
30. Annenberg and Gallup Research, 1984.
31. Ron Sellers "Nine Global Trends in Religion," *The Futurist,* January/February 1998, 20–25.
32. Michael Warren, *Communication and Cultural Analysis* (Bergin and Garvey, 1992), 3.
33. Ibid., 2.
34. Ibid., 3.
35. Ibid., 32.
36. Bernard Haring, "Theologie der Kommunikation und theologische Meinungs-bildung," F. J. Eilers, et al., *Kirche und Publizistik. Dreizehn Kommentare zur Pastoralinstruktion Communio et Progessio* (F. Schoningh, 1972), 38.
37. Parker Palmer, *The Courage to Teach* (Jossey-Bass, 1998), 151.
38. John Catoir, "Cardinal Suenens calls for a new Pentecost" *America,* 6 June 1987.
39. Edward Schillebeeckx, *The Language of Faith* (Orbis, 1995).

CHAPTER 2

1. The idea of "supercity" is taken from John Naisbitt's *Megatrends,* which connects the future of Asia with the success of megalopolis.
2. Jacques Séguéla, *Vote au-dessus d'un nid cocos* (Flammarion, 1992).
3. *Asia Focus* 11 July 1997, 11.
4. Charles Baudelaire, "Bénédiction" in *Les Fleurs du Mal.*
5. *Asia Focus,* 1995.
6. M. Légaut, whom I was able to interview many times, marked in depth my reflec-tion on the Gospel and communication. See in particular *L'homme à la recherché de son humanité,* Aubier, 1971. Interviews on cassettes *Initiation à la lecture de l'Évangile; La sagesse de l'âge; Le sermon sur la montagne,* (Novacom/Crec Avex).
7. C. G. Jung, *Man Discovering Himself* (Payot, 1966), 398.
8. *Le Monde,* 10–13 July 1997, citing Arnaud Pateyron and Robert Salmon, *Les nou-velles technologies de l'information et l'Enterprise* (Economica, 1996).
9. Jeremy Rifkin, *The End of Work,* from the French translation *La Fin du travail* (La Découverte, 1996).
10. *Courier International,* 11 May 1995.
11. *Courier International,* 22 February 1996.
12. Georgia Tech Research Corporation cited in *Planet Internet,* July/August 1997, 67.
13. Gerard Lohfink, *L'Église ue voulait Jésus* (Le Cerf, 1985).
14. Eugen Drewermann, *La Parole Qui Guerit* (Le Cerf, 1991), 16.
15. Martin Achard in *Vocabulaire Biblique* (Delachaux et Niestle, 1956), 174.
16. Yasyshi Inoué, *Confucius* (Stock, 1993).

CHAPTER 3

1. Pierre Babin and Marshall McLuhan, *Autre homme, autre chretian a l'ere electron-ique* (Chalet, 1977).
2. Milan Kundera, *L'Immortalité* (Gallimard, 1990), 301.
3. Pierre Babin, *Langage et culture des médias* (Ed. Universitaires, 1991), 25–41.
4. Ibid., 25.
5. C. G. Jung, *Man and His Symbols* (Laffont, 1964), 20.
6. Pierre Babin with Mercedes Iannone, *The New Era in Religious Communication* (Fortress, 1991).
7. Dominique Wolton, *Penser la communication* (Flammarion, 1997), 248.

CHAPTER 4

1. Emmanuel Arnaud Pateyron and Robert Salmon, *Les nouvelles technologies de l'information et l'Enterprise* (Economica, 1996).
2. Dominique Wolton, *Penser la communcation* (Flammarion, 1997), 246, 250.
3. Pateyron and Salmon, op. cit., 64–65.
4. Ibid.
5. Ibid.
6. Wolton, op. cit., 267.
7. Ibid.
8. Marshall McLuhan, *Pour comprendre les Media* (Marne/Seuil, 1968).
9. This conversation emerged from a session of pilot research at the Jesuit Center of Puskat at Yogyakarta, Indonesia.
10. Bill Gates, *The Road Ahead* (Penguin, 1996).

CHAPTER 5

1. *Libération,* 13 July 1997, 40.
2. Jacques Séguéla, *Vote au-dessus d'un nid de cocos* (Flammarion, 1992), 111.
3. Albert Mehrabian cited in Babin's *Langage et culture des medias,* 25.
4. Cardinal Martini, *Communication et Spiritualité* (Chalet, 1991), 19.
5. Regis Debray, *Cours de médiologie générale* (Gallimard, 1991), 93–94.
6. The survey is published in the magazine *La Vie,* 24 April 1997.
7. Emmanuel Arnaud Pateyron and Robert Salmon, *Les nouvelles technologies de l'information et l'Enterprise* (Economica, 1996), 25.

CHAPTER 6

1. The Bishop of Reims was speaking to Cardinal Martini, archbishop of Milan, who had come for three days to our center, CREC-AVEX, to reflect on communications with his team of journalists and pastoral ministers.
2. Raimundo Panikkar, "Le défi chrétien du troisème millénaire," letter 37 in the bulletin *Afrique & Parole,* September 1993.
3. *San Francisco Chronicle,* 20 June 1997, 12.
4. Michael Amaladoss, *À la rencontre des cultures* (Atelier, 1997), 29–30, 38.
5. Unpublished conversation with Pierre Babin.
6. Derrick de Kerckhove, *Connected Intelligence: The Arrival of the Web Society* (Somerville House, 1997).
7. Paul Ricoeur, philosopher, on the Jean-Marie Cavada radio program, "The Year 2000 is already begun," *The March of the Century,* 13 March 1996.

CHAPTER 7

1. On all of these subjects, see Pierre Babin, *New Era in Religious Communications* (Fortress, 1991), 114.

CHAPTER 8

1. Karl Rahner, *The Great Church Year* (Crossroad, 1995), 7.
2. James Bacik, *The Gracious Mystery* (St. Anthony Messenger Press, 1986), 2.
3. *Webster's II New Riverside University Dictionary,* (Houghton Mifflin, 1984), 432.
4. Congregation for the Clergy, *General Directory for Catechesis* (United States Catholic Conference, 1997).

5. V. Bailey Gillespie, *The Dynamics of Religious Conversion: Identity and Transformation,* (Religious Education Press 1991), 26.

6. Ibid., 25.

7. Walter Conn, *Christian Conversion: A Developmental Interpretation of Autonomy and Surrender* (Paulist Press, 1986), 212.

8. Synod for Oceania, Working Paper. http://www.catholic.org.au/frames/what snew/ilsasbo.htm, 22 September 1998.

9. James Griffin, *Pastoral Letter on Evangelization,* 1992, Diocese of Columbus, Ohio, USA. In *Origins* 21, no. 4 (6 June 1991).

10. *Go and Make Disciples,* National Conference of Catholic Bishops, 19 November 1998, in *Origins* 423.

11. Griffin, op. cit.

12. Special Synod for America. The Working Paper. In *Origins* 27, no. 13 (September, 1997), 206.

13. Ibid.

14. Definition taken from William Reiser, "Inculturation and Doctrinal Development," *Heythrop Journal* 22 (1981): 135.

15. John Paul II, "The African Bishop's Challenge," Address to the Bishops of Kenya, 7 May 1980, *Origins* 10, no. 2 (29 May 1980): 29.

16. See Avery Dulles, *The Reshaping of Catholicism* (Harper & Row, 1988), 34–50.

17. See Karl Barth, *The Epistle to the Romans* (Oxford University Press, 1977), 267–68.

18. See Paul Tillich, *Systematic Theology* (University of Chicago Press, 1951), 1: 7.

19. The celebration of the Fifth Centenary of Evangelization in the Americas caused problems for Native Americans, African Americans, and others in the United States. These groups questioned the reason for celebration when reconciliation and healing might be more appropriate. They challenged the Church to rethink the concept and process of indigenization and enculturation of the Gospel.

20. Paul VI, Address to the Bishops of the African Continent, 31 July 1969. See *L'observatore romano,* 1 August 1969.

21. See Raimundo Panikkar, "Theology in a Culturally Diverse World," in *Pluralism and Oppression* (University Press of America, 1991), 6.

22. Archbishop Ikenago of Osaka, Japan. Synod of Asia, 21 April 1998. *Origins* 27, no. 46 (7 May 1998): 770.

23. Vincent Donovan, *Christianity Rediscovered,* 2nd ed. (Orbis Books, 1983), 144-45.

24. Synod of Bishops Special Assembly for Oceania. "Jesus Christ and the People of Oceania: Walking His Way, Telling His Truth, and Living His Life." Working Document. (Vatican, 1998), Article no.22. http://www.vatican.com.

25. James J O'Donnell, *Avatars of the Word: From Papyrus to Cyberspace* (Harvard University Press, 1998), 9.

26. Mary Catherine Hilkert, "Preaching," in *The New Dictionary of Catholic Spirituality,* ed. Michael Downey (Liturgical Press, 1993), 775.

CHAPTER 9

1. Robert Wuthnow, *Christianity in the Twenty-First Century* (Oxford University Press, 1993), 5.

2. Peter C. Brinckerhoff, *Mission-Based Marketing* (Alpine Guild, 1997).

3. Ibid., 47.

4. Aylward Shorter, *Christianity and the African Imagination* (Paulines Publications Africa, 1996), 119.

5. The application of the principles of adaptation and apperception is not new to the catechetical or evangelizing efforts of the twentieth century. Sr. Rosalie Walsh, MHSH, in her historical contribution to catechetics called *The Adaptive Way of*

Teaching Confraternity Classes (Catechetical Guild, 1955), clearly demonstrated these principles in her methodology for teaching religion. These principles remain critical and relevant to our ministries today as in the past.

6. Rebecca Leet, *Marketing for Mission* (National Center for NonProfit Boards, 1998).
7. Ibid., 4.
8. Norman Shawchuck, Philip Kotler, Bruce Wrenn, and Gustav Rath, *Marketing for Congregations: Choosing to Serve People More Effectively* (Abingdon, 1992), 60.
9. Javier Perez de Cuellar, *Our Creative Diversity* (UNESCO, 1995), 105.
10. Karl Rahner, *The Great Church Year* (Crossroad, 1995), 9.

CHAPTER **10**

1. The ideas adapted in this section are gleaned from the works of Joel Barker. A series of his publications and video productions have influenced these insights, in particular his book *Future Edge* (Morrow, 1992) and the video *Paradigm Principles* (CRM Films, California).
2. Joel Barker, *Tactics of Innovation,* CRM Films, 1998.
3. Robert M. Tomasko, *Rethinking the Corporation: The Architecture of Change* (Amacon, 1993), 182.
4. Arturo Bastes, *Asian Formation for Consecrated Life.* Synod for Asia 1998. *Origins* 27, no. 46 (7 May 1998): 775.
5. Ibid., 776.
6. Leo Jun Ikenago, Synod for Asia 1998. *Origins* 27, no. 46 (7 May 1998), 770.
7. Aylward Shorter, *Christianity and the African Imagination.* (Paulines Publications Africa, 1996), 123.
8. Ibid.
9. *Pastoral Communications Planning* (USCC/NCCB, 1997).
10. Bill Capodagli and Lynn Jackson, *The Disney Way* (McGraw-Hill, 1998).
11. Barbara C. Sampson, "Technology for Education," *TERC,* 21, no. 2 (Fall 1998): 1–2.
12. Stephen D. O'Leary, "Cyberspace as Sacred Space: Communicating Religion on Computer Networks" *Journal of the American Academy of Religion* (Fall 1996), LIX no. 4, 797.
13. Jeff Zaleski, *The Soul of Cyberspace,* (HarperSanFrancisco, 1997).
14. Sherry Turkle, *The Second Self: Computers and the Human Spirit* (Granada, 1984).
15. Rob Shields, ed., *Cultures of Internet* (Sage, 1996), 129.
16. Sherry Turkle, *Life on the Screen* (Touchstone, 1997).